すべての日本人に贈る —— 「話すため」の英文法

一億人の英文法 CDブック

ENGLISH GRAMMAR FOR 100 MILLION JAPANESE

東洋学園大学 教授
大西泰斗
Hiroto Onishi

麗澤大学 教授
ポール・マクベイ
Paul Chris McVay

はじめに

INTRODUCTION

みなさんこんにちは。「一億人の英文法」著者の大西泰斗です。この『一億人の英文法 CD ブック』は，出版以来たくさんの方々にご希望いただき実現した企画です。

話すことのできない英語に価値はありません。僕たちはネイティブの意見にハイハイとうなずくために英語をやっているわけじゃないんだからね。彼らと対等に話し合い，ビジネスや友情を広げていく。「話せる英語」それが目標。

みなさんは「一億人の英文法」ですでに文法を制覇しました。話すための英語に大きく踏み出したのです。あとは，このCD ブックでせっかくの文法力を話す力にスムーズにつなげるだけ。

がんばって。もうすぐだよ。

2012年6月

大西泰斗

P. C. McVay

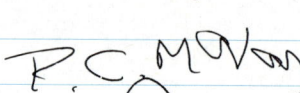

本書の使い方

HOW TO USE

　『一億人の英文法』は「話す」を目標に据えた初めての英文法書です。その執筆で僕が常に心掛けたのは，すべての形のなかにある意味とリズムをあきらかにすること。聴くため・読むためだけの英語なら，some も several も a number of も「いくつか」でいいかもしれません。「it は仮主語でほんとーの主語は to 以下です」レベルの理解でも役に立つのかもしれません。だけどね。「話す」となったらそんな理解は役に立ちません。語感に根ざした深い理解が必要なのです——ってここまでは，みなさん十分ご理解いただいていますよね？

　さて本題。
　『一億人の英文法』で深い理解はできたといっても，会話の臨戦態勢が整ったというわけではありません。理屈も語感も十分なみなさんには，もう１つ越えていただきたい壁があるのです——それは「理屈と語感」を内在化させること。すぐに取り出せる感覚として体のなかに収めることです。
　会話は話し手を待ってはくれません。いくら正しく理解していても，some か several を選ぶのに２秒も３秒もかかるのでは使いものにはなりません。それは文作りでも同じこと。「授与」が感じられれば「授与型」が，it で文を始めたら後ろから「追いかける」to 不定詞や節が，意識せずとも瞬時に出てこなければ，スムーズな会話などできません。
　そこでこの「CD ブック」。
　本教材には，『一億人の英文法』で使った重要例文（カコミ付きで大きく表示された例文）がすべて音声化されています。この CD を使ってみなさんがやらなければならないことは，ただ１つ。音読と暗唱です。
　ただね，ただ漫然と音読していてもダメ。ただ丸暗記はダメ。その文が，その形が，その単語が，ネイティブと同じキモチで・同じ気安さで出ている

かに心をくだきながら徹底的に音読・暗唱するのです。いつ何時話しかけられても，その形が使える自信ができるまで繰り返すのです。もし理解が不十分なら，本に戻って確認することも忘れないでくださいね。

　さあ，はじめましょう。

　ネイティブの感覚を熟知した数百の文を暗唱しても日常会話すらできない――英語はね，そんなにハードルが高いことばじゃないんですよ。

　がんばれ。

【音声学習の四原則】　※詳細はCD冒頭で大西泰斗先生が解説します。

❶ 単に英文を聞き流すのはやめる
❷ しっかりと声を出して音読する
❸ 英文を作り出す過程を意識する
❹ 無意識にできるまで繰り返す

※1つの例文が読まれたあと，同じ英文が「小さい音」でもう1回繰り返されます。この小さい音声に合わせてしっかり音読しましょう。

例　(通常音声) I like English.　(小音声) I like English.　(通常音声) The boy hates dogs.　(小音声) The boy hates dogs.

　Ohnishi-sensei has explained clearly what this CD is about and how best to use it. Now I'd like to give you a few tips about how to practice the example sentences. It is obviously not good enough to simply read the sentences aloud as if they were simply collections of words. This is not the way to make your English more fluent and natural.

　So, what is the best way to practice? Well, you have to practice with HEART. That means you have to listen very carefully to each example sentence and repeat each one exactly as you hear it. Not just word by word, but going beyond the words, capturing the true meaning of each sentence. And how can you do that? Well, I have a simple 3-point method that will help you. I call it the IFS (I F S) method.

　First, I. This stands for IMAGINE. You must imagine the situation in as much detail as possible. Where are you, who is there, what is happening? JUMP into the situation and live it! Next, F. This stands for FEEL. Once you're inside the situation, you must FEEL the emotion of the situation. Happiness, sadness, excitement, boredom, curiosity, whatever … Just get in touch with the feeling of the particular situation. Finally, S. This stands for SPEAK. Now you're ready to open your mouth and SPEAK.

　So, the IFS method means that IF you imagine the situation, and IF you feel the emotion of that situation, and IF you wait until you've completed these 2 steps before you speak, your English conversation will be far more natural and impactful.

　So, get ready. No more robotic repetition of sentences! Put heart into your English and … practice, practice, practice!

Paul Chris McVay

もくじ

CONTENTS

PART 1　英語文の骨格
- CHAPTER 1　主語・動詞・基本文型　P.9
- CHAPTER 2　名詞　P.25

PART 2　修飾
- CHAPTER 3　形容詞　P.47
- CHAPTER 4　副詞　P.51
- CHAPTER 5　比較　P.57
- CHAPTER 6　否定　P.65
- CHAPTER 7　助動詞　P.71
- CHAPTER 8　前置詞　P.81
- CHAPTER 9　WH修飾　P.85

PART 3　自由な要素
- CHAPTER 10　動詞 -ING 形　P.95
- CHAPTER 11　TO 不定詞　P.99
- CHAPTER 12　過去分詞形　P.107
- CHAPTER 13　節　P.113

PART 4　配置転換
- CHAPTER 14　疑問文　P.121
- CHAPTER 15　さまざまな配置転換　P.131

PART 5　時表現
- CHAPTER 16　時表現　P.137

PART 6　文の流れ
- CHAPTER 17　接続詞　P.157
- CHAPTER 18　流れを整える　P.163

MEMO

ENGLISH GRAMMAR FOR 100 MILLION JAPANESE

PART 1
英語文の骨格
FRAMEWORKS OF ENGLISH

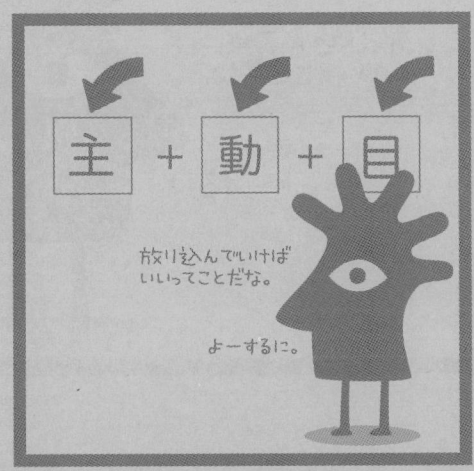

CHAPTER 1：主語・動詞・基本文型
CHAPTER 2：名詞

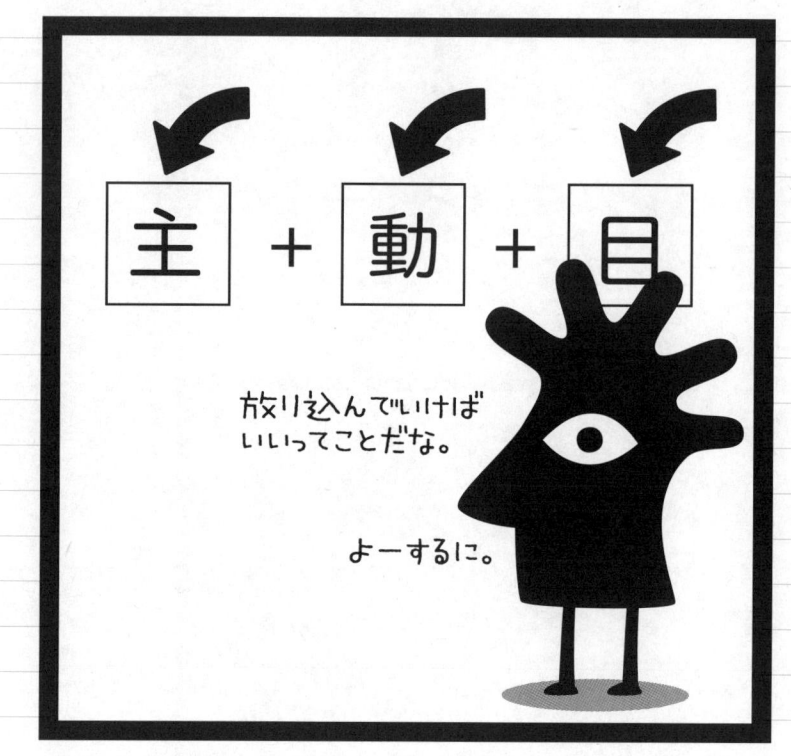

英語は配置のことば。主語の位置に放り込めば，何でも主語として生き生きと動き出します。動詞の位置なら動詞。で，動詞の後ろに名詞をいくつ配置するかによって，文の型が決まります。スロットに放り込むつもりで並べていくんだよ。

PART 1
CHAPTER 1

主語・動詞・基本文型

SUBJECTS, VERBS, BASIC SENTENCE PATTERNS

英語例文数：107　　CDトラック数：10

PART 1 · CHAPTER 1：主語・動詞・基本文型

SECTION 1 主語

CD track **A-02**

A「主語」とは？ (☞P.50) ←このページ数は本書のページ数ではなく、本体『一億人の英文法』のページ数です。(以下同)

[a] I like English.

[b] The boy hates dogs.

B 主語のつかまえ方 (☞P.51)

[a] My American friend loves natto.

[b] The guy surrounded by girls over there must be Dan. He's so popular.

C 主語の「資格」は特にない (☞P.52)

[a] The music teacher blew his top in class today.

[b] My friend's dog peed on my foot!

[c] Brad's birthday party was awesome.

D 無生物主語 (☞P.55)

[a] The news made us all excited.

[b] The sign says you can't swim in this lake.

ⓒ My Gothic Lolita clothes cost a fortune.

ⓓ This road takes you to the stadium.

ⓔ Her good looks actually hurt her acting career.

PART 1 · CHAPTER 1：主語・動詞・基本文型

動詞

CD track **A-03**

A 動詞の基礎知識（2種類の動詞）（☞P.56）

[a] We are happy.

[b] I like dogs.

[c] Are you happy? / He isn't[is not] happy.

[d] Do you like dogs? / I don't[do not] like dogs.

B 動詞の変化形（☞P.57）

■ 現在形

[a] I am a student.

[b] You are very kind.

[c] Ken is so smart!

[d] Ken and Mary are in the schoolyard.

[e] I play soccer every day.

[f] My son plays soccer at school.

[g] He has a wonderful family.

■ 過去形

[a] I was really happy.

[b] They were sad.

[c] I played soccer yesterday.

[d] He played in the All Japan High School Soccer Tournament last year.

■ -ing 形

[a] He is playing soccer at the moment.

[b] The girl playing soccer with the boys is Manami.

[c] Playing soccer is a lot of fun.

■ 過去分詞形

[a] He is good! He surely has played soccer before.

[b] Soccer is played by over 240 million people.

[c] The sport played by most people? That's soccer!

PART 1 - CHAPTER 1：主語・動詞・基本文型

基本文型① 他動型

CD track **A-04**

A 他動型 （☞P.66）

[a] **My boyfriend kissed my sister!**

[b] **Some students teased the new teacher.**

[c] **Ellie has beautiful eyes.**

[d] **I know Monet.**

基本文型② 自動型

CD track A-05

A 自動型 (☞P.69)

a My brother swims really fast.

b My baseball team didn't play well last night.

B 前置詞とのコンビネーション (☞P.69)

a I looked at the girl.

b Are you going to the school festival?

PART 1 - CHAPTER 1：主語・動詞・基本文型

基本文型③ 説明型

CD track **A-06**

A 説明型（be動詞）（☞P.71）

a My cousin is a delinquent kid.

b My cousin is very moody.

c My cousin is at the bowling alley.

C 説明型（一般動詞）（☞P.74）

a Many workers have become jobless.

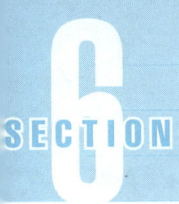

基本文型④ 授与型

CD track A-07

A 授与型 (☞P.77)

[a] I gave the guy my cell phone number.

[b] My parents bought me an iPad.

[c] We wrote our teacher thank-you poems.

[d] I wonder who sent me this Valentine card.

[h] My old scooter costs me a lot of time and money.

[i] It took me 3 hours to get home from school today, owing to the typhoon.

[j] The hotel charged us $50 for losing our room key!

B 授与をあらわす，もう１つの形 (☞P.78)

[a] She gave this love letter to me.
[She gave me this love letter.]

PART 1 - CHAPTER 1 : 主語・動詞・基本文型

目的語説明文

CD track A-08

A 目的語説明文（基礎）（☞P.86）

a Just call me Ken.

b Everyone believed him a genius.

c He smashed the lock open.

d I consider him trustworthy.

B 知覚をあらわす動詞と共に（☞P.88）

a I saw Mary cross the street.

b Didn't you hear the phone ring?

C make, have, let と共に（☞P.89）

a I'll do anything to make you happy.

b The story made me sad.

c When I was on homestay, I found it difficult to make myself understood in English.

d Shall we have our new plasma TV on the wall?

[e] I had my uniform cleaned for the graduation ceremony.

[f] I had my iPod pinched from my school bag.

[g] Don't let me down.

[h] The PE teacher made the students run in the snow.

[i] I'll have the nurse bandage your leg for you.

[j] My daughter's upset because I won't let her get a tattoo.

D to 不定詞を説明語句に (☞P.93)

[a] My parents always tell me to study harder!

[b] Why don't you ask the ALT to help you with your English?

[c] I'll try to persuade my Dad to give us a ride.

[d] Of course I want her to go out with me, but she's not interested.

[e] My parents won't allow me to stay out after midnight.

[f] Thank goodness they've gone. I didn't expect them to stay so long.

PART 1 · CHAPTER 1 ： 主語・動詞・基本文型

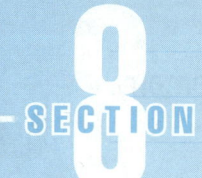

レポート文

CD track A-09

A レポート文基礎：that 節 （☞P.95）

[a] I think Mary is gorgeous.

[b] Tom said today is his birthday!

[c] Mom doesn't understand that I want to live my own life.

[d] Tom said to me he loved me.

[e] He promised me he would try his best from now on.

[f] I'm afraid we cannot give you a refund.

[g] I'm so sad he lost his job.

[h] Sorry I'm late!

B whether/if 節・wh 節での展開 （☞P.98）

[a] I didn't know whether/if you had already paid the bill.

[b] Clare asked me whether/if I have a key to the safe.

[c] We haven't decided whether/if we'll go to Malaysia this summer.

[e] I didn't know where I could get tickets for the concert.

[f] Does anyone know when the baseball camp begins?

[g] The teacher explained why bullying is bad.

[h] I don't have a clue how they did it.

C 遠回し疑問文（☞P.100）

[a] Tell me what kind of music you like.

[b] This is my country's national dish. I wonder if you'll like it.

[c] Do you know where the nearest convenience store is?

D コミュニケーション動詞のクセ（☞P.102）

[a] She says she isn't going to marry him.

[b] I hear that the PTA is going to hold a fund-raising concert next month.

[c] Kaori tells me that Kenji is going to be expelled from school.

PART 1 - CHAPTER 1：主語・動詞・基本文型

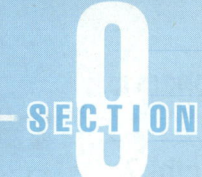

命令文

CD track **A-10**

A 命令文の形・意識 （☞P.103）

[a] **Concentrate!**

[b] **Be more confident.**

B 禁止の命令・勧誘 （☞P.104）

[a] **Don't speak to me like that again, OK?**

[b] **Don't be nervous. You'll be fine.**

[c] **Let's order pizza tonight.**

[d] **No, let's not order pizza tonight.**

[e] **Let's order pizza tonight, shall we?**

SECTION 10 There 文

CD track **A-11**

主語・動詞・基本文型

A there 文の形・意識 (☞P.108)

ⓐ **Mommy, there is a strange-looking guy at the door.**

B 2とおりの「〜がある・いる」 (☞P.109)

ⓐ **Tom is in the park. (× There is Tom in the park.)**

ⓑ **Your son is in the school yard at the moment.
(× There is your son ...)**

ⓒ **He was in the car park.
(× There was he in the car park.)**

MEMO

PART 1

CHAPTER 2

名詞
NOUNS

英語例文数：179　CDトラック数：04

PART 1 - CHAPTER 2：名詞

可算名詞・不可算名詞

CD track **A-12**

A 可算・不可算の判断 （☞P.135）

[a] I have a cat, but I hate dogs.

[b] In summer, my dad drinks beer every night.

C 不可算名詞の「数え方」 （☞P.140）

[a] Could I have a cup of coffee, please?

[b] Two glasses of cola, please.

[c] Eh? You ate 4 pieces of cake?

[d] This tank holds about 50 liters of gasoline.

D 可算・不可算は臨機応変 （☞P.142）

■[1] 可算・不可算の違いで大きく意味が異なる名詞

[a] The suspicious parcel was wrapped in brown paper.

[b] Your idea is great on paper, but it'll never work in practice.

[c] I saw the ad in a paper.

■② モノの「状態」

[a] **Look at the size of those pumpkins!**

[b] **How much pumpkin did you put in the soup?**

[d] **This is a fish.**

[e] **This is fish.**

■③ モノに対する「見方」

[a] **How many cakes did you eat?**

[b] **How often do you eat cake?**

[c] **Two buses came at the same time.**

[d] **I go to school by bus.**

[e] **You can fill out the form in pen or pencil.**

[f] **There are several excellent schools in the city.**

[g] **All children should have the right to go to school.**

[h] **We all drank a lot of wine at the barbecue.**

[i] **New World wines have become hugely popular.**

[j] **Indonesia produces excellent coffee.**

[k] Three coffees, please.

[l] Our gourmet shop offers a wide variety of flavored coffees.

■[4] 見えないモノを区別する

[a] My neighbors were making so much noise I couldn't sleep.

[b] Shh! I can hear a strange noise coming from the engine.

[c] Conversation requires skill.

[d] I had an interesting conversation with my ex last night.

単数名詞・複数名詞

CD track **A-13**

A 単数形・複数形の作り方（規則変化）(☞P.151)

[a] I need 6 volunteers.

[b] I met 2 girls from Australia last night.

B 単数ととらえる・複数ととらえる (☞P.154)

■1 集団をあらわす名詞の単数・複数

[a] He comes from a large family.

[b] There are 2 Indian families living near us.

[c] My family are/is all into skiing.

■2 「the ＋形容詞（〜の人々）」は複数扱い

[a] I just read a surprising article about the homeless in Tokyo.

[b] Is it natural for the strong to protect the weak?

■3 まとめて考える場合は単数扱い

[a] 20 cigarettes is a lot to smoke in a day, don't you think?

[b] 20 miles is a long way to run.

■4 2つ以上のモノが絡む動作は複数

[a] **Did you get a direct flight or did you have to change planes?**

[b] **Some people bow while others shake hands.**

[c] **I made friends with Karen.**

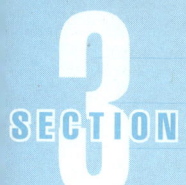

限定詞

CD track **A-14**

A 限定詞なしの名詞 (☞P.160)

■① ～というもの

ⓐ Crows are highly intelligent birds but also a big nuisance!

ⓑ I like wine.

■② リストアップ

ⓐ We need poster paper, marker pens, and glue. — How about scissors?

B the (☞P.162)

■① 文脈から1つに決まる

ⓐ I met Karen's boyfriend last night. The guy is not friendly at all.

ⓑ You know I bought a new iPod? Well, the thing keeps freezing up!

■② その場の状況から1つに決まる

ⓐ Close the door!

ⓑ Look at the puppy over there! Cute, isn't it?

PART 1 - CHAPTER 2：名詞

■③ 常識から１つに決まる

ⓐ 70% of the earth's surface is covered by water.

ⓑ The world is our classroom.

ⓒ Which way is the restroom?

■④ 「１つ」を意味に含む語句

ⓐ Chiaki Mukai was the first Japanese woman to travel into space.

ⓑ You are the only girl I've ever loved.

ⓒ Who is the youngest of the three?

■⑤ 「the ＋ 複数」＝１つに決まるグループ

ⓐ Look at the penguins over there.

ⓑ The Yamadas are moving to Indonesia.

■⑥ the のネイティブレベル

ⓐ Sharon is the woman for the job.

ⓑ I think the Hotel de Paris is the place to stay.

ⓐ John plays the flute and the clarinet.

ⓑ I love listening to you playing the piano.

[e] The police were quickly on the scene.

[f] I don't often listen to the radio.

[g] Do you prefer the town or the country?

[h] I want to live in a house on the river[beach / golf course].

[i] I'll pop into the supermarket/bank on my way home from work.

[j] You'd better take him to the hospital.

[k] I think you should see the doctor.

[n] The American husband never complains about his wife.

[o] The British gentleman is hard to find these days.

[a] The poor are getting poorer, and the rich are getting richer.

[b] It's natural for the young to be rebellious, isn't it?

[a] This is the present that he gave me.

[b] You can use the phone in my office.

[c] She told me the reason why she left him.

C a[an] (☞P.172)

[a] I'd like a chocolate donut. — Just one, please.

■① 話題に初めて登場させる

[a] You know I bought a new iPod? Well, the thing keeps freezing up!

[b] Karen's got a new boyfriend. The guy is not friendly at all.

■② 特定のモノを思い描いていない

[a] I need to find a part-time job.

[b] Mary is a nurse.

■③ a の類推

[a] This is a present that he gave me.

[b] She gave me a reason why she left him.

D some (☞P.178)

■① ボンヤリと意識

[a] There are some squirrels in your garden.

[b] I need some olive oil for the salad.

■② 温かい some

[a] Would you like some coffee?

[b] Do you need some assistance?

E any (☞P.181)

■① 何でも・誰でも・どれでも

[a] Any parent would want the best for their child.

[b] He's more talented than any player I've coached.

[c] Choose any card.

■② 疑問文での any

[a] Do you have any other questions?

[b] Do you have any money?

■③ 否定文での any

[a] I don't like any sports.

[b] I don't need any advice, especially from you!

■④ 条件節での if

[a] If you need any more information, just let me know.

[b] If you want any sleep, don't stay at that hotel — it has a disco!

F all, every, each (☞P.183)

■① all：ひっくるめて「全部」

ⓐ **All the spectators were delighted.**

ⓑ **I've been a musician all my life.**

■② every：緻密な「すべて」

ⓐ **Every participant will receive a prize.**

ⓑ **I hope every customer is satisfied.**

ⓒ **Every mother looks after her children.**

■③ each：それぞれ

ⓐ **She had a glass of wine in each hand.**

ⓑ **In golf, each player keeps their own score.**

G no (☞P.187)

ⓐ **Nobody came to my party!**

ⓑ **I looked everywhere, but I found nothing.**

ⓒ **No problem. I'll fix it in no time.**

H both, either, neither (☞P.188)

① both

ⓐ **Both my kids are excellent swimmers.**

ⓑ **I love the puppy and the kitten. Can I have both, Mom?**

② either

ⓐ **You can invest in stocks or property, but either way it's risky.**

ⓑ **I have a blue sweater and a red one — you can borrow either.**

③ neither

ⓐ **It was a deal in which neither side got what it really wanted.**

ⓑ **Do you take milk and sugar? — Neither, thanks.**

I 数量表現 (☞P.190)

① 多い

ⓐ **I don't have many friends.**

ⓑ **Do you have much rain in October?**

② 少ない

ⓐ **I have a few good friends.**

ⓑ **I have little time for exercise these days.**

J 指示の this, that (☞P.196)

■① this (この) と that (あの)

[a] **What do you think about this bag?**

[b] **Whose is that red sports car over there?**

■② 単独で使う this, that

[a] **This is a really nice apartment.**

[b] **Didn't you know that?**

[c] **My situation is quite different from that of the rest of my family.**

[d] **Some of the best wines are those from the New World.**

[e] **Good friends are those who stick together through thick and thin.**

K 単独で使える限定詞 (☞P.198)

[a] **Excuse me. Do you sell batteries? — Yes, but we don't have any at the moment.**

[b] **How much are these lamps? — Each costs 25 dollars.**

c I'm looking for Velcro tape. — I'm afraid we have none at the moment.

d I must buy some milk because I don't have much.

e Which do you want? — I'll take both.

f What do you think of these designs? —Mmm ... I like this, but I hate that.

g How many computers do you have? — I have three.

h I don't like any [most / many / one] of these paintings.

i None of my friends sent me a birthday card.

j Neither of them can cook.

PART 1 - CHAPTER 2 : 名詞

SECTION 4　代名詞

CD track **A-15**

A 代名詞の基本（☞P.201）

ⓐ **I want to talk about Mayuko. Is she ready to become a team leader?**

ⓑ **Steve and Lee are coming tonight. They are very interesting guys.**

ⓒ **What's that? — It's a crystal paperweight.**

ⓓ **What are those? — They are crystal paperweights.**

B 主格の使い方（☞P.203）

ⓐ **He is a dentist.**

ⓑ **John is taller than I.**

C 所有格の使い方（☞P.203）

ⓐ **His arms are bigger than my thighs!**

ⓑ **Every country has its own traditions and customs.**

ⓒ **Your Mom's cherry pie is simply the best!**

D 目的格の使い方 (☞P.207)

[a] **I love him.**

[b] **I went fishing with them.**

E 所有代名詞の使い方 (☞P.207)

[a] **Is this your tennis racket? — No, that's mine on the bench.**

[b] **Whose motorbike is that over there? — It's Barry's.**

[c] **I met an old friend of mine on my way home tonight.**

F -self 形の使い方 (☞P.208)

[a] **Helen cut herself chopping carrots.**

[b] **He often talks to himself.**

[c] **I have to do everything myself.**

G it (☞P.209)

■1 文脈に登場したもの・内容を受ける it

[a] **What is that? — It's a can opener.**

[b] **How did you like the movie? — I liked it a lot.**

[c] I'm really sorry. It won't happen again.

[d] This is going to be a fantastic event. There's no doubt about it.

[e] And another thing. You should … — OK, OK, I got it.

■[2] 状況を受ける it

[a] It's dark here.

[b] How's it going, Chris?

[c] It's fine today.

[d] It's Wednesday today.

[e] What time is it? — It's 11 o'clock.

[f] It's 5 kilometers from here to the station.

■[3] it + to 不定詞／節

[a] It is difficult to speak English.

[b] It takes less than 7 hours to get to Singapore.

[d] It is surprising (that) he agreed to this deal.

[e] It's up to you whether/if you take him back (or not).

[f] It's still not clear when the election results will be announced.

■[4] it ～ that ... の強調構文

[a] It was my little sister that stepped on the cat yesterday.

■[H] 人々一般をあらわす代名詞 (☞P.217)

[a] You need a visa to travel to China.

[b] We shall fight terrorism all the way.

[c] They say life begins at 40.

[d] People always want what they cannot have.

[e] One should never take love for granted.

■[I] 前に出てきた単語の代わりをする one (☞P.218)

[a] My cell phone is broken, so I need to buy a new one.

[b] My brother bought an iPod, so I got one too.

[c] Which is your daughter? — The one with the ponytails.

[d] What kind of guys do you like? — Ones with a good sense of humor.

PART 1 - CHAPTER 2：名詞

J 固有名詞 (☞P.220)

a. Mr. Jones arrived in Tokyo, Japan, on Wednesday, September 26th. Japan is a country known for its global companies like Sony, Honda, Toyota and so on. He decided to visit Japan after reading Ruth Benedict's *The Chrysanthemum and the Sword*.

b. She is the Martha Stewart of Japan.

c. I would love to own a Maserati.

d. There are two Lucys in our class.

e. The Nancy I know is a nurse.

ENGLISH GRAMMAR FOR 100 MILLION JAPANESE

PART 2
修飾
MODIFICATION

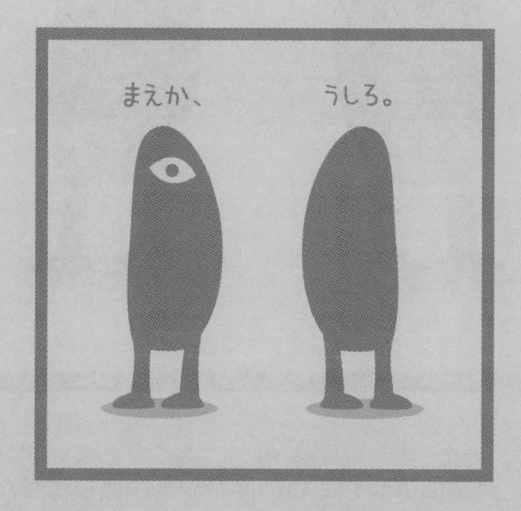

CHAPTER 3：形容詞
CHAPTER 4：副詞　　CHAPTER 5：比較
CHAPTER 6：否定　　CHAPTER 7：助動詞
CHAPTER 8：前置詞　CHAPTER 9：WH修飾

配置のことば，英語にはややこしい修飾規則はありません。前か後ろ。前は限定，後ろは説明（限定ルール・説明ルール）。とくに説明ルールは，とっても使いでがありますよ。説明は後追い。どんどん後ろから付け足す。いいね！

PART 2
CHAPTER 3
形容詞
ADJECTIVES

英語例文数：30　　CDトラック数：03

学習日
| 1回目 | 2回目 | 3回目 | 4回目 | 5回目 |

PART 2 - CHAPTER 3：形容詞

SECTION 1　前から限定

CD track **A-16**

A 限定する （☞P.234）

a Look at the cute girl over there.

b This guy with a goofy face asked me out. I just laughed!

c These rotten eggs stink!

B 重ねて修飾 （☞P.234）

a Mark is an excellent though reckless driver.

b Naomi is a bright but lazy student.

c Look at that beautiful silk top.

d I have a 5-year-old daughter.

e This is an amazing, once-in-a-lifetime opportunity. You gotta take it!

SECTION 2 後ろから説明

CD track A-17

A 説明を加える (☞P.237)

[a] My girlfriend is gorgeous.

[b] She is beautiful and kind.

[c] My parents were strict but fair.

B 説明を加えるその他の例 (☞P.238)

[a] I'm looking for somebody better.

[b] I've tried everything possible.

[c] This is the worst scenario imaginable.

[d] I'm afraid there are no seats available for tonight's show.

[e] I was given a bag full of cookies!

[f] That building is 150 meters high and 35 meters wide.

[g] Did you know that the tallest man in the world is 2 meters 49 centimeters tall?

[h] You have to be 17 years old to drive a car in England.

[i] The Great Seto Bridge is 13.1 kms long.

PART 2 - CHAPTER 3 : 形容詞

SECTION 3　何でも形容詞

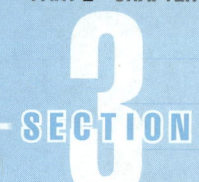

CD track **A-18**

A 名詞による修飾（☞P.242）

[a] We have to do everything to prevent child abuse.

[b] Hey, he's just a child. Go easy on him.

B 動詞 -ing 形で修飾（☞P.242）

[a] His smile is warm and very inviting.

[b] What you just said is interesting.

[c] There are many English-speaking countries.

C 過去分詞形で修飾（☞P.243）

[a] Written English is sometimes different from spoken English.

[b] He is not well-known as an artist yet, but he will be one day.

[c] I love coming here in the off-season because the beaches are deserted.

D -ing 形 vs 過去分詞形（感情をあらわす）（☞P.244）

[a] That game was really exciting.

[b] I was really excited watching that game.

PART 2
CHAPTER 4
副詞
ADVERBS

英語例文数:29　CDトラック数:02

PART 2 - CHAPTER 4：副詞

SECTION 1　説明の副詞

CD track A-19

A 時をあらわす副詞（☞P.250）

[a] I walked my dog yesterday.

[b] I had a party last night.

[c] Wake me up at 6:30, Mom.

B 場所をあらわす副詞（☞P.251）

[a] Many people were waiting at the bus stop.

[b] Terrible things happened here.

C「どのように」「どれくらい」—様態をあらわす副詞（☞P.253）

[a] We ran really fast and just managed to catch the last train.

[b] The player scored with his hand, not with his head!

[c] I beat my best time for the 100 meters by 0.8 seconds.

[d] You'd better do exactly as I tell you, or you'll be in big trouble.

D 副詞の重ね方 (☞P.254)

ⓐ The couple argued bitterly in the restaurant last night.

ⓑ The barbecue will start around 1 o'clock tomorrow.

ⓒ We first met at the Louvre in Paris.

PART 2 - CHAPTER 4：副詞

SECTION 2 限定の副詞

CD track **A-20**

A 限定一般（☞P.257）

[a] These shoes are ridiculously expensive.

[b] The tea was steaming hot.

[c] You stole it just because your mates told you to?

[d] I was bad-mouthing Jim and he was standing right behind me!

[e] You can use cell phones only in this area.

[f] He almost/nearly missed his flight.

[g] I kind of love her.

[h] We hardly talk anymore.

B 程度副詞（☞P.259）

[a] He is so annoying.

[b] That is totally out of the question.

C 頻度副詞（☞P.261）

ⓐ **My Mom always nags me.**

ⓑ **I never talk back to my wife.**

D 確信の度合いをあらわす副詞（☞P.264）

ⓐ **We will definitely make it on time.**

E 評価・態度をあらわす副詞（☞P.266）

ⓐ **Happily, no one was badly injured.**

ⓑ **Clearly, we cannot handle this situation alone.**

ⓒ **Honestly, I have no idea where she went.**

ⓓ **As far as I know, John is the only one with a key to the safe.**

MEMO

PART 2
CHAPTER 5
比較
COMPARISON

英語例文数: 54　　CDトラック数: 03

学習日
| 1回目 | 2回目 | 3回目 | 4回目 | 5回目 |

PART 2 - CHAPTER 5：比較

SECTION 1 同等レベルをあらわす

CD track A-21

A as-as の基本（☞P.283）

[a] Tom is as tall as Mary. （←Tom is tall.）

[b] She now speaks as naturally as a native speaker.
（←She now speaks naturally.）

B 限定語句と共に as-as を使う（☞P.285）

[a] She isn't as attractive as Sarah.

[b] He didn't play as well as his opponent, so he lost.

[d] He is almost as tall as his Dad now.

[e] Why did he get the job rather than me? I'm just as experienced as him.

[f] This cake is not half as delicious as it looks.

[g] Facebook is more than twice as big as MySpace. Soon it may be three times as big!

C as-as を使い切る（☞P.287）

[a] I have as many CDs as Ken.

[b] She is not as good at skiing as me.

[c] Eva didn't perform as well in the exam as Tess.

[d] I think reading a book is as exciting as going to Disneyland.

[e] To write Japanese is not as easy as to speak Japanese.

[f] On camp, I ate as well as at home.

[g] My boss isn't as decisive as he was a couple of years ago.

[h] Dad is not as grumpy as he used to be.

[i] I don't skip as many classes as you do!

[j] Chris isn't as old as he looks.

[k] His first album sold over half a million copies, and we hope this second album will be just as popular (as that).

[l] Hiromi plays the piano brilliantly, but her sister can play as well (as her).

PART 2 - CHAPTER 5：比較

SECTION 2　比較級表現：「より〜」

CD track **A-22**

A 比較級の基本 (☞P.299)

[a] Follow me. This way is quicker.
（←This way is quick.）

[b] Many people would like to have a better life.
（←Many people would like to have a good life.）

[c] Try swinging the bat more slowly.
（←Try swinging the bat slowly.）

[d] Slow down! I can't keep up with you. ― That's because I'm fitter than you.

[e] How can I get a higher TOEIC score than her? She lived in the States for 5 years!

[f] C'mon, kids! You can scream louder than that.

B 限定語句と共に比較級を使う (☞P.301)

[a] Camembert is not tastier than Gruyère.

[b] My kids are no naughtier than most other children.

[c] This perfume isn't any more fragrant than the one I

am using now.

[d] My hair is a little[a bit] softer than before, so I like this conditioner.

[e] Today's test was somewhat more difficult than last week's.

[f] Fruit is much[a lot] cheaper in my country than in Japan.

[g] Whisky is far stronger than beer.

[h] My brother is even crazier than me!

[i] Sue is 3 years younger than me.

[j] I need 3 more volunteers.

[k] Did you know that a woman's hips are approximately one and a half times bigger than a man's?

[l] This new operating system is 2 to 3 times faster than the old one.

[C] 比較級を使い切る (☞P.303)

[a] It's cheaper to eat at home than at a restaurant.

PART 2 - CHAPTER 5 : 比較

[b] Doing something is always better than doing nothing.

[c] It's healthier to play sport than to watch it on TV.

[d] He looks older than he actually is.

[e] I'm more confident than I've ever been.

[f] The meeting lasted longer than I expected.

SECTION 3 最上級表現:「最も〜」

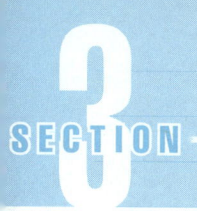

CD track **A-23**

A 最上級を使った基本型 (☞P.310)

[a] Cheryl is the cleverest. (←Cheryl is clever.)

[b] Oh, that's the best idea. (←Oh, that's a good idea.)

[c] Which engine runs the most efficiently?
(←Which engine runs efficiently?)

[d] Tom is the tallest of the three/of all.

[e] Tom is the tallest in his class.

B 最上級を限定語句と共に使う (☞P.312)

[a] This is by far the best book we've written.

[b] This site has the very best free online games.

[c] Her grades are excellent, but they are only the second best.

C 最上級の応用型:「これまで」とのコンビネーション (☞P.313)

[a] This is the most moving film I've ever seen.

[b] This is the most hair-raising roller-coaster ever created.

PART 2

CHAPTER 6

否定

NEGATION

英語例文数：26　　CDトラック数：03

PART 2 - CHAPTER 6：否定

SECTION 1 not は前から

CD track A-24

A 否定文の作り方 (☞P.317)

■① 助動詞あり

[a] I can't play the piano.

[b] You mustn't cheat in the test.

[c] I won't let you down.

■② 助動詞なし (do + not)

[a] Most kids don't like jazz.

[b] He doesn't speak English.

[c] He didn't erase his private data.

■③ be動詞

[a] I'm not happy.

[b] They weren't sophisticated.

B 語句を否定する (☞P.320)

[a] Who let the cat out of the bag? ― Not me!

[b] This apartment is not for rent.

c. He'll win not because he's the better player but because he's stronger mentally.

d. I was fired for not being punctual.

e. I worked hard not to have credit card debt.

PART 2 - CHAPTER 6：否定

SECTION 2 「強い単語」とのコンビネーション

CD track **A-25**

[a]-1 **I don't really like your new car.**

[a]-2 **I really don't like your new car.**

[b]-1 **My girlfriend is not always on time.**

[b]-2 **My girlfriend is always not on time!**

SECTION 3 — not のクセ

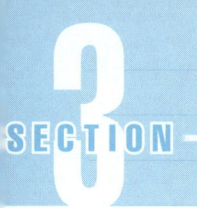

CD track **A-26**

A 「思う」文で前倒し （☞P.324）

[a] I don't think it's right.

[b] I don't believe we've met.

C not を含んだ文に対する受け答え：not を明示する （☞P.326）

[a] You're not leaving me, right? — Of course not!

[b] I didn't go to work today. — Why not?

D 文の代わりに not （☞P.327）

[a] Did you manage to get tickets for tonight's game? — I'm afraid not.

[b] Do you think it will rain tomorrow? — I hope not.

[c] Have you finished your homework? — Not yet.

[d] I'm afraid I've been wasting your time. — Not at all.

[e] I should be able to fix it by tomorrow. If not, you'll have to wait till Monday.

MEMO

PART 2
CHAPTER 7

助動詞

AUXILIARY VERBS

英語例文数：57　　CDトラック数：08

PART 2 - CHAPTER 7：助動詞

SECTION 1 助動詞基礎

CD track **A-27**

A 疑問文と否定文（☞P.334）

[a] **Can she speak English?**

[b] **She cannot speak English.**

B 助動詞の変化形（☞P.335）

[a] **Next week I will be able to [× can] give you more information.**

[b] **I want to be able to [× can] play golf like Ryo Ishikawa!**

[c] **I enjoy being able to [× canning] play sports again.**

SECTION 2 主要助動詞の意味① MUST

CD track A-28

A ～しなければならない（義務）(☞P.336)

[a] I must get back home by midnight. My parents will be mad if I don't!

[b] The boss is really strict about deadlines, so you must finish the report on time.

B ～しちゃダメ（禁止）(☞P.337)

[a] You mustn't[must not] do that! You'll lose all your data.

C ～しなくちゃいけないよ（強いおすすめ）(☞P.337)

[a] You must go see Tokyo Sky Tree. It's amazing!

D ～にちがいない（強い確信）(☞P.337)

[a] The injury isn't serious? You must be relieved.

[b] You won a scholarship to study abroad? You must be delighted.

PART 2 - CHAPTER 7：助動詞

主要助動詞の意味② MAY

SECTION 3

CD track **A-29**

A ～してよい（許可）(☞P.339)

[a] You may smoke only in the designated area.

[b] May I take your order?

B ～してはいけません（禁止）(☞P.340)

[a] You may not take photographs inside the museum.

C ～しますように（祈願）(☞P.340)

[a] May all your dreams come true!

[b] I hope that she may find the courage to face this tough challenge.

D ～かもしれない（推量）(☞P.341)

[a] We may go skiing in Hokkaido this winter.

[b] There are so many exciting countries to visit. I may go to Malaysia, or Singapore, or then again I may go to Indonesia. I'm just not sure yet.

SECTION 4 主要助動詞の意味③ WILL

CD track **A-30**

A ～だろう（予測）（☞P.343）

[a] You will feel much better tomorrow.

[b] You will soon get the hang of it, if you concentrate hard.

[c] I've tried to convince him, but he won't change his mind.

B ～するものだ（法則・習慣）（☞P.344）

[a] Accidents will happen.

[b] A true friend will stick by you in good times and bad.

[c] My boyfriend's funny. He will spend hours in front of his computer and forget I'm even there!

C ～するよ（意志）（☞P.345）

[a] I've left my wallet at home. — Don't worry. I'll lend you some money.

[b] I WILL marry him, Dad!　※WILLは強く発音されています。

主要助動詞の意味④ CAN

SECTION 5

PART 2 - CHAPTER 7：助動詞

CD track **A-31**

A ～できる（能力）（☞P.346）

a Junko can speak English.

b Come on! You can do it.

B ～していい（許可）（☞P.347）

a You can borrow my racket, if you like.

b Can I use your car, Dad?

c Can I help you?

C ～しうる・ときに～することもある（潜在的な性質）（☞P.348）

a My boss can be so selfish at times.

b Saitama can be very hot.

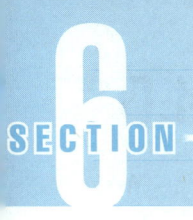

SECTION 6 主要助動詞の意味⑤ SHALL

CD track A-32

A 法律（☞P.350）

a **You shall not steal.**

b **Neither slavery nor involuntary servitude ... shall exist within the United States, or any place subject to their jurisdiction.**

B 必ず〜になる（確信）（☞P.351）

a **We shall all die.**

b **We shall never forget your kindness.**

c **You shall regret this!**

C Shall I 〜？・Shall we 〜？（〜しましょう）（☞P.351）

a **Shall I help you?**

b **Shall we dance?**

PART 2 - CHAPTER 7：助動詞

主要助動詞の意味⑥ SHOULD

SECTION 7

CD track **A-33**

A 〜すべき（義務・アドバイス） (☞P.353)

a. You're always broke. You should be more careful with your money.

b. You should definitely get an iPhone. They're great.

c. You should watch your weight.

B 〜はず（確信） (☞P.354)

a. That should be no problem.

b. I should be able to get to the restaurant by 7.

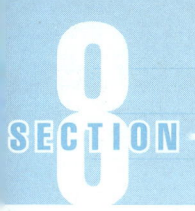

SECTION 8 助動詞相当のフレーズ

CD track **A-34**

A have to （☞P.360）

■① 〜しなくてはならない（義務）

[a] You have to have your hair cut.

[b] You have to send your resume and a cover letter.

[c] We may have to cancel our trip because grandmother is very ill.

■② 〜にちがいない（強い確信）

[a] She has to be the culprit.

[b] This has to be the happiest day of my life.

B be able to （☞P.363）

[a] I'm able to speak 4 languages.

[b] I was able to catch the last train.

[c] I've always wanted to be able to speak Japanese fluently.

PART 2 - CHAPTER 7：助動詞

C had better/had best ＋ 動詞原形 (☞P.365)

[a] **You'd better call the ambulance!**

[b] **You'd best not snitch on us, or we'll beat you up.**

D used to (☞P.366)

[a] **There used to be a movie theater right here.**

[b] **I used to get into trouble all the time when I was a kid.**

PART 2

CHAPTER 8

前置詞

PREPOSITIONS

英語例文数：23　　CDトラック数：02

PART 2 - CHAPTER 8：前置詞

SECTION 1 　前置詞基礎

CD track A-35

A 前置詞の位置と働き （☞P.369）

ⓐ There's an apple on the table.

ⓑ Come and have some fun with us.

■ 前置詞句（前置詞＋名詞）の働き

ⓐ There are a lot of Brazilians in Japan.

ⓑ I can't sleep at night.

ⓒ The tropical depression is headed towards the Bahamas.

ⓓ I can pick a lock with a paper clip.

ⓔ All the kids in my class donated money to the Haiti Disaster Relief Fund.

■ 前置詞の目的語になる要素

ⓐ Our situation went from bad to worse.

ⓑ He lived in Paris until quite recently.

ⓒ The cat came out from under the sofa.

[d] She insulted me by calling me a liar.

[e] Your success depends on how you make decisions.

[f] It's a bit awkward to invite Helen to the party in that her ex is also coming.

PART 2 - CHAPTER 8：前置詞

SECTION 2　前置詞の選択

CD track **A-36**

ⓐ Unbelievable! Apples are selling at just ¥200 a kilo.

ⓑ I bumped into Cathy at the bank this morning.

ⓒ Their flight is due to arrive at 10 a.m.

ⓓ Mommy, look at my drawing.

ⓖ We had to change planes at Heathrow Airport.

ⓗ We enjoyed some last-minute shopping in Heathrow Airport.

ⓙ My Dad often sits in his favorite chair and watches TV all night.

ⓚ My Dad usually sits on that chair.

ⓛ My ball hit a tree and landed in the fairway. Lucky!

ⓜ When I played golf in Thailand, there were monkeys on the fairway!

PART 2
CHAPTER 9

WH修飾

WH-MODIFICATION

英語例文数：46　　CDトラック数：06

PART 2 - CHAPTER 9：WH 修飾

SECTION 1　人指定の who

CD track **B-01**

A 主語の穴に組み合わせる （☞P.416）

[a] The woman who lives next door is an English teacher.

[b] I know a lot of teenagers who feel alone.

B 目的語の穴に組み合わせる （☞P.417）

[a] That is the guy who I met on the flight to London.

[b] The girl who I wanted to date is now going out with my best friend!

[c] Is that the teacher who you complained about?

C 「whose＋名詞」の形 （☞P.418）

[a] A widower is a man whose wife has died.

[b] I just met a girl whose brother I used to play soccer with.

SECTION 2 モノ指定の which

CD track B-02

A 主語の穴に組み合わせる （☞P.421）

a. Where is the parcel which arrived this morning?

b. The house which was for sale has now been sold.

c. I like stories which have happy endings.

B 目的語の穴に組み合わせる （☞P.422）

a. The top which Ann bought is sooo cute!

b. The engagement ring which I want is too expensive.

c. Is this the file which you are looking for?

C 「whose ＋ 名詞」の形 （☞P.422）

a. You can choose a laptop whose price falls within your budget.

b. This is a smartphone whose new features are simply amazing.

PART 2 - CHAPTER 9：WH 修飾

SECTION 3　wh語を使わないケース・thatを使うケースなど　CD track B-03

A wh語を使わないケース （☞P.424）

[a] The car I want to get is eco-friendly.

[b] The guy you were talking to is my boyfriend.

B that を使うケース （☞P.425）

[a] The woman that lives next door is an English teacher.

[b] The car that I want to get is eco-friendly.

[c] Man is the only animal that blushes.

[d] The simplest emotion that we discover in the human mind is curiosity.

[e] This is everything that I own.

[f] Don't believe all the stuff that you read in the papers.

SECTION 4 where, when, why の wh修飾

CD track B-04

A 「場所」の where （☞P.429）

ⓐ This is the park where I go jogging every morning.

ⓑ Kochi is the city where Sakamoto Ryoma was born.

ⓒ I'd like to live in a city where there is a great nightlife.

B 「時間」の when （☞P.430）

ⓐ Can you pinpoint the moment when you fell in love with her?

ⓑ The exact time when the murder was committed is still unknown.

ⓒ The Christmas when the whole family got together remains one of my fondest memories.

C 「理由」の why （☞P.431）

ⓐ The reason why I'm calling you is to ask you a favor.

ハイレベル wh修飾

CD track B-05

A 深く埋め込まれた穴 (☞P.433)

[a] This is the video game that most of the kids in my school say is just awesome.

[b] The keys which my wife thought I lost were in her bag.

[c] The people I really wanted to be at my party can't come.

SECTION 6 カンマ付 wh修飾

CD track B-06

A カンマ付 wh修飾は注釈を加える (☞P.435)

[a] The woman who designed my apartment is a Feng Shui expert.

[b] My brother Geoff, who is a chef, lives in Newcastle.

B カンマ付 wh修飾の実践 (☞P.436)

[a] Jim, who speaks French, works as a tourist guide.

[b] We stayed at the Grand Hotel, which some friends recommended to us.

[c] Amy, whose date had just stood her up, was in a foul mood.

[d] I'm going to spend two weeks in New York, where my daughter lives.

[e] The students gave an excuse for missing class, the truth of which was dubious, to say the least!

[f] This watch, for which I paid 200 dollars, is a fake!

[g] I bought 2 kilos of apples, half of which were rotten!

[h] We looked at 2 apartments, both of which were excellent.

[i] She was adventurous, which he was not.

[j] I had to play the piano in front of the whole school, which was really nerve-wracking.

[k] If he ever went out on the town, which didn't happen very often, he usually came home drunk.

ENGLISH GRAMMAR FOR 100 MILLION JAPANESE

PART 3
自由な要素

FREE ELEMENTS

CHAPTER 10：動詞-ING形
CHAPTER 11：TO 不定詞
CHAPTER 12：過去分詞形
CHAPTER 13：節

英語は配置で機能（品詞）が決まることばです。主語や目的語の位置に置けば名詞として働き，名詞の前後に置けば形容詞，動詞句の後ろにおけば副詞として働きます。-ing，to 不定詞，過去分詞，節を使いこなすポイントは，これらパッケージ表現の置き場所に注意することだけ。配置原則の総仕上げでもあるこのパート，がんばっていこー。

PART 3
CHAPTER 10
動詞-ING形
-ING FORM

英語例文数：20　　CDトラック数：02

PART 3 - CHAPTER 10：動詞-ING形

SECTION 1　名詞位置での動詞-ing形

CD track **B-07**

A 主語として（☞P.445）

[a] Making new friends is not so easy.

[b] Talking in the library is prohibited.

B 目的語として（☞P.445）

[a] I like playing video games with my buddies.

[b] Stop picking your nose!

C 前置詞の目的語として（☞P.446）

[a] My kid sister is great at dancing hip-hop.

[b] I'm proud of being bicultural.

[c] I got the booby prize for coming last in my club's golf tournament.

SECTION 2　修飾位置での動詞-ing形

CD track B-08

A 説明型の-ing形（進行形）（☞P.447）

[a] My brother is acting like an idiot — as usual!

[b] Lucy is putting on her make-up.

B 名詞句の説明（☞P.448）

[a] The man scolding those 2 boys is the headmaster.

[b] The woman driving the bus is my sister-in-law.

C 目的語説明（☞P.448）

[a] Sorry to keep you waiting.

[b] His jokes had the entire audience rolling in the aisles.

[c] I saw your girlfriend getting into a taxi with a tall, good-looking guy!

D 動詞句の説明（☞P.449）

[a] The player fell to the ground clutching his ankle.

[b] I've spent all morning cleaning up after the party.

PART 3 - CHAPTER 10：動詞-ING形

[c] I was busy sweeping up the fallen leaves.

E 文の説明 (☞P.450)

[a] He broke his collarbone playing rugby on Saturday morning.

[b] A huge hurricane hit the city, causing untold destruction.

[c] She left a note on the door, finding nobody home.

PART 3
CHAPTER 11
TO 不定詞
TO-INFINITIVES

英語例文数：42　　CDトラック数：04

PART 3 - CHAPTER 11 : TO 不定詞

SECTION 1 名詞位置での to 不定詞

CD track **B-09**

A 主語として（☞P.455）

a To make new friends is not so easy.

b To talk in the library is prohibited.

B 目的語として（☞P.457）

a I like to play video games with my buddies.

b I want to be a policeman.

SECTION 2 修飾位置での to 不定詞①

CD track **B-10**

A come/get ＋ to 不定詞　(☞P.460)

ⓐ He came to appreciate his parents.

ⓑ We got to know Tokyo very well.

B 説明型の to 不定詞　(☞P.461)

ⓐ To see is to believe.

ⓑ Our goal is to find a cure for AIDS.

ⓒ If you are to get her back, you need to do more than just apologize.

ⓓ You are all to be here by 7 a.m. sharp, understood?

ⓔ 4 kids from Liverpool were to form the most famous rock band in the world.

ⓕ The President is to visit Japan next week.

ⓖ The flight attendant seems/appears to be stressed out.

ⓗ Her prediction turned out to be right.

[i] His plan proved to be successful.

[j] We happened to be wearing the same dress!

C 目的語説明 (☞P.463)

[a] I thought him to be an honest person.

[b] I consider him to be open-minded.

[c] I found her to be a most capable assistant.

SECTION 3　修飾位置での to 不定詞②

CD track **B-11**

A 動詞句の説明と「足りないを補う」（☞P.464）

ⓐ I'm going to Egypt to do some scuba diving.

ⓑ I was excited to hear about your new project.

ⓒ He grew up to be a famous architect.

ⓓ She must be out of her mind to walk around such a dangerous area alone.

B 名詞句の説明（☞P.467）

ⓐ I don't have the right tools here to fix your bicycle.

ⓑ Michelle was the first female golfer to play in a men's tournament.

ⓒ I need someone to drive me to the station.

C 形容詞の説明（☞P.468）

ⓐ He is easy[hard / difficult / impossible] to fool.

ⓑ She is sure[certain / likely / unlikely] to lose her cool.

c． The new recruits are eager to show their worth.

D wh語 ＋ to 不定詞 (☞P.469)

a． I have no idea what to say.

b． Tell me when to start.

c． I know where to find them.

d． Could you tell me which way to go for the post office?

SECTION 4 to 不定詞が使われるその他の形

CD track **B-12**

A 「it + to 不定詞」のコンビネーション (☞P.471)

[a] It's difficult to get up in the morning.

[b] It's tough for the unemployed to make ends meet.

[c] I find it difficult to get up early.

[d] I thought it wise to let you know in advance.

B too ～ to ... (～すぎて…できない) (☞P.472)

[a] I was too shocked to speak.

C to + 完了形 (☞P.473)

[a] It was good to have reserved seats.

[b] She pretended to have been working.

D to 不定詞の否定 (☞P.474)

[a] It would be crazy not to accept their offer.

[b] We'll try not to make too much noise.

MEMO

PART 3
CHAPTER 12

過去分詞形
PAST PARTICIPLES

英語例文数：42　　CDトラック数：03

PART 3 - CHAPTER 12：過去分詞形

SECTION 2 　受動文基礎

CD track **B-13**

A 受動文の基本型 （☞P.481）

ⓐ John was attacked by the dog.

ⓑ 100 students were chosen for their leadership qualities.

B 受動文のあらわす「時」・疑問文・否定文 （☞P.482）

ⓐ Smoochy is buried in the pet cemetery.

ⓑ We have been invited to Pat's New Year's party.

ⓒ Our school cafeteria is being renovated.

ⓓ Your report must be typed, not handwritten, OK?

ⓔ Tokyo Sky Tree will be completed in 2011.

ⓕ When was this school established?

ⓖ The fans were not pleased with their team's performance this evening.

SECTION 3 受動文のバリエーション

CD track **B-14**

A 授与をあらわす受動文 （☞P.486）

[a] Mary was given a trophy.

[b] I was offered the job, but I turned it down.

[c] A trophy was given to Mary.

[d] A love letter was handed to the teacher.

B 目的語説明の受動文 （☞P.487）

[a] I think the guy was called Peter, but I can't be sure.

[b] Her nails were painted bright pink.

[c] Two students were seen necking in an empty classroom.

C to 不定詞と受動文のコンビネーション （☞P.488）

[a] I was asked to make a speech at my ex-student's wedding.

[b] We were all told to stay calm.

12 ▼ 過去分詞形

PART 3 - CHAPTER 12：過去分詞形

[d] One of last year's Nobel Prize winners is thought to be in jail.

[e] Her new book is expected to become an immediate bestseller.

[f] Jericho is said to be the oldest city in the world.

[g] The hostages are reported to be in good health.

D 句動詞の受動文 (☞P.491)

[a] My kids have been brought up to respect their elders.

[b] The match has been called off.

[c] The big event will be talked about for years.

[d] Don't worry. The tickets have already been paid for.

SECTION 4 過去分詞で修飾

CD track **B-15**

A be動詞以外の説明型で用いる過去分詞 (☞P.492)

[a] Your mom looked disgusted when she saw my tattoos!

[b] They became frightened.

[c] John got arrested for harassment.

B 目的語修飾 (☞P.493)

[a] Keep the door locked.

[b] Would you like your fish grilled?

[c] We found two windows smashed.

[d] I thought I heard my name called.

[e] It's difficult to make myself heard over all this noise.

[f] I got my car washed yesterday.

C 過去分詞，その他の修飾 (☞P.494)

[a] The man pictured in the newspaper article is my grandfather.

[b] The things stolen from my room were not very valuable.

[c] My daughter came home disappointed.

[d] We arrived at our destination exhausted.

[e] The fans left the stadium overjoyed.

[f] Our situation is healthy, compared with many companies.

[g] This apartment is ideal for young couples, situated very close to lots of shops, restaurants, and leisure facilities.

PART 3
CHAPTER 13

節
CLAUSES

英語例文数：23　　CDトラック数：02

PART 3 - CHAPTER 13：節

SECTION 1　主語位置での節

CD track B-16

A タダの節 (☞P.499)

[a] That he is hiding something is plain to see.

[b] That she was only after his money was obvious to everyone.

B 二択の whether 節 (☞P.500)

[a] Whether our plan will work or not is in the lap of the Gods!

[b] Whether we buy the house will depend largely on the selling price.

C wh節 (☞P.500)

[a] What the government decides affects all of us.

[b] When she gets married is her business.

[c] Where she got all that money from is a mystery.

[d] How you treat others will determine how others treat you.

[e] Who my son goes out with doesn't concern me at all.

[f] Why he has so much trouble finding a girlfriend is beyond me.

修飾語位置での節

CD track B-17

A 説明型の節 (☞P.502)

ⓐ The simple fact is that we lost the game. End of story.

ⓑ The question is whether/if our business can survive or not.

ⓒ This is where I hang out.

B 動詞(句)を説明(レポート文) (☞P.502)

ⓐ I love that I live within walking distance of my university.

ⓑ He told me that he doesn't want to lose me.

ⓒ I'm afraid that your plan doesn't work.

ⓓ I don't know whether I can afford to go clubbing this weekend.

ⓔ He asked me if I wanted to go to Guam with him.

ⓕ I asked her what she was planning to wear to the wedding.

g. He didn't tell me what kind of restaurant he would like to go to.

h. I don't have a clue where I put my keys.

C 名詞句の説明 (☞P.504)

a. I heard a rumor that you had dumped your boyfriend. So what about me?

b. The question whether an afterlife exists has been debated for centuries.

MEMO

ENGLISH GRAMMAR FOR 100 MILLION JAPANESE

PART 4
配置転換
DISLOCATION

CHAPTER 14：疑問文
CHAPTER 15：さまざまな配置転換

PART 4　配置転換

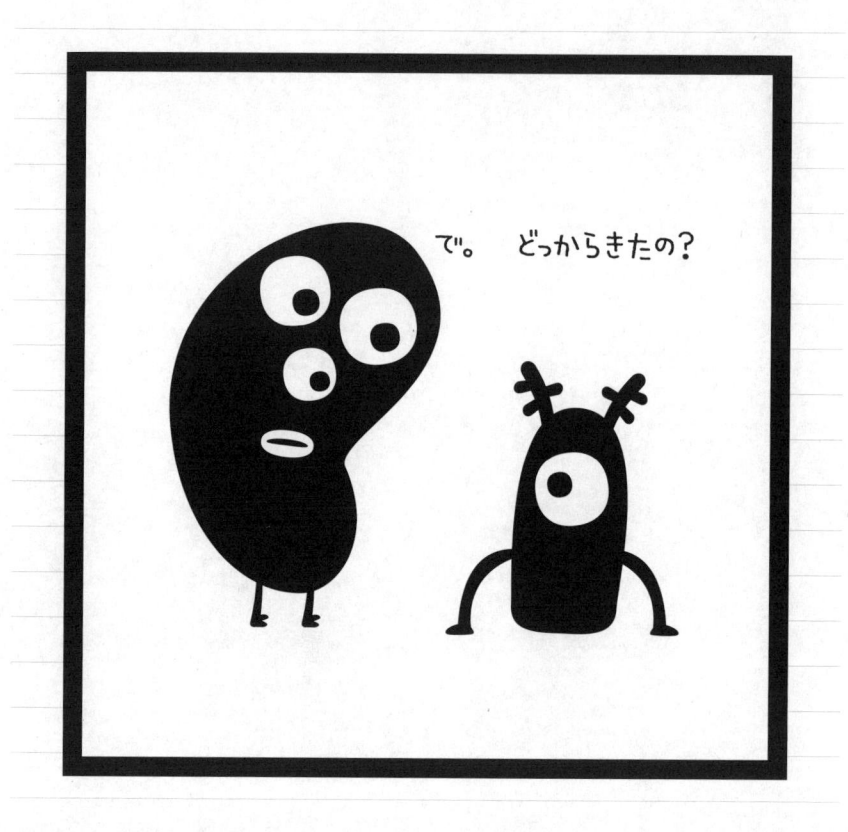

配置のことば英語では，配置の変更は感情・意図を伴います。疑問文も感嘆文も，規則であーゆー形になっているわけではありません。しっかりと感情を通わせながら音読することが肝心ですよ。

PART 4
CHAPTER 14
疑問文
QUESTIONS

英語例文数 63　　CDトラック数 07

PART 4 - CHAPTER 14：疑問文

SECTION 1　基本疑問文

CD track **B-18**

A 助動詞あり（☞P.513）

a **Can you click your fingers?**

b **Should I dump him?**

c **Have you read my e-mail?**

B 助動詞なし（☞P.514）

a **Do you speak English?**

b **Does he speak English?**

c **Did he speak English?**

C be動詞（☞P.514）

a **Are you happy?**

b **Was he happy?**

SECTION 2 否定疑問文

CD track B-19

A 否定疑問文の作り方 (☞P.517)

[a] Can't you find a job?

[b] Don't you love me?

[c] Isn't this disgusting?

PART 4 - CHAPTER 14：疑問文

SECTION 3　付加疑問文

CD track **B-20**

A 付加疑問文の基本 （☞P.518）

ⓐ You can play golf better than me, can't you?

ⓑ So, Sayuri doesn't want to go out with me, does she?

ⓒ It's a beautiful day, isn't it?

B ちょこっとくっつけるテクニック （☞P.519）

ⓐ You remembered to bring the key, right? ― Er...!

ⓑ Get off my back, OK?

ⓒ So, you fancy my girlfriend, huh?

ⓓ That's a good idea, don't you think?

ⓔ Quit pestering me, will you?

ⓕ Let's break for lunch, shall we?

SECTION 4　あいづち疑問文

CD track B-21

A 発言を受ける疑問文 （☞P.522）

[a] I can give you a ride, if you like.
　　— Oh, can you?　That would be great!

[b] I never wear any make-up.　— Oh, don't you?

[c] I'm a bit drunk.　— Oh, are you?

PART 4 - CHAPTER 14：疑問文

SECTION 6

wh疑問文② 基礎

CD track **B-22**

A wh疑問文の基礎 （☞P.525）

[a] What do you like? — I like hamachi.

[b] Who did you meet? — I met Hanako.

[c] Which do you like, dogs or cats? — I like cats.

[d] Whose is this car? — It's my Dad's.

B 「時・場所・方法・理由」を尋ねる場合 （☞P.526）

[a] When do you work out? — I work out every morning.

[b] Where do you live? — I live in Urawa.

[c] How did you come here? — I came here by car.

[d] Why didn't you come? — Because I had a terrible cold.

C 前置詞の目的語を尋ねる （☞P.527）

[a] What did you do that for?

[b] Who are you going drinking with?

D 主語を尋ねる (☞P.528)

[a] **Who told you that?** — A little bird did!

[b] **What makes you happy?** — Hanging out with my friends does.

E 「大きな」wh語 (☞P.528)

[a] **How old are you?** — I'm seventeen (years old).

[b] **How tall are you?** — I'm 5 foot 8.

[c] **How much is this?** — It's $5.

[d] **How many CDs do you have?** — Too many to count!

[e] **What kind of music do you like?** — I like rap music best.

[f] **Whose rollerblades are those?** — They're my brother's.

wh疑問文③ 応用

CD track **B-23**

A レポート文内を尋ねる（☞P.530）

a Who did you say called Cindy?

b Who did you say Cindy called?

c What do you think was the cause of the accident?

d Who do you suppose was behind the fraud?

e When do you imagine you'll get the results of the scan?

B その他の複雑なwh疑問文（☞P.531）

a What time do you want me to come round?

b Where in the whole world would you choose to go for your honeymoon?

c Who would you like to be as famous as?

C wh語を使った聞き返し（☞P.532）

a I went to Estonia. — You went where?

ⓑ I bought a loofah. — You bought what?

ⓒ I've been a vegetarian for 20 years. — You've been a vegetarian for how long?

疑問ではない疑問文

A 依頼の疑問文 (☞P.533)

[a] Can you talk some sense into my son? He won't listen to me. — Well, I can try!

[b] Will you call me as soon as you get there? I'll be worried about you. — Sure, Mom.

B 疑問の意味ではない疑問文 (☞P.534)

[a] Why don't you stay a little longer?

[b] Why don't we take the kids to the zoo on Saturday?

[c] Why must you always leave the toilet seat up?

[d] What do you say we go catch a movie tonight?

[e] Would you like a cup of coffee?

[f] How/What about going for a bike ride along the river?

[g] Who are you to give me advice?

[h] Who do you think you are?

[i] You need to apologize to her. — Why should I?

PART 4
CHAPTER 15

さまざまな配置転換

Various Types of Dislocation

英語例文数：18　　CDトラック数：02

PART 4 - CHAPTER 15：さまざまな配置転換

SECTION 1　主語―助動詞倒置

CD track B-25

A（主語―助動詞）倒置形の活用：基本 （☞P.536）

a Oh, man. Am I angry!

b Did I put my foot in my mouth!

c I love banana pancakes. ― So do I!

d I've not seen his latest movie yet. ― Neither have I.

B 否定的語句 + 倒置 （☞P.537）

a Never have I seen such terrible behavior!

b Rarely have I laughed so hard.

c Little did they know how tough this challenge was going to be.

d No sooner had I entered the interview room than I knew I had no chance.

C 仮定法 + 倒置 （☞P.539）

a Had he not braked so quickly, he would have run over the child.

[b] Had there not been a doctor nearby, my son might have died.

[c] Were I to lose my job, we would have enough to survive for a year or two.

[d] Were it not for Bill, there would be no soccer club.

D Should + 倒置 (☞P.540)

[a] Should you incur any additional costs, we'll reimburse you.

[b] I've repaired everything, and it's working fine now, but should there be a problem, just bring it back, OK?

PART 4 - CHAPTER 15：さまざまな配置転換

SECTION 2 — 感嘆文・その他

CD track **B-26**

A 感嘆文 （☞P.541）

[a] What a nice camera you have!

[b] How fast he runs!

B その他の配置転換 （☞P.542）

[a] In class she is as quiet as a mouse, but at karaoke she is wild!

[b] Last night, I had a big fight with my boyfriend.

ENGLISH GRAMMAR FOR 100 MILLION JAPANESE

PART 5
時表現
TEMPORAL EXPRESSIONS

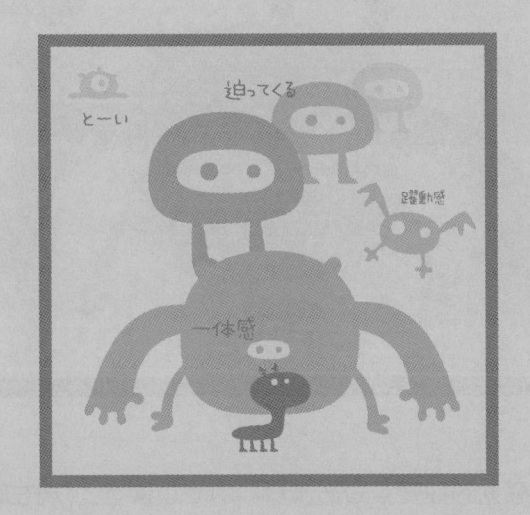

CHAPTER 16：時表現

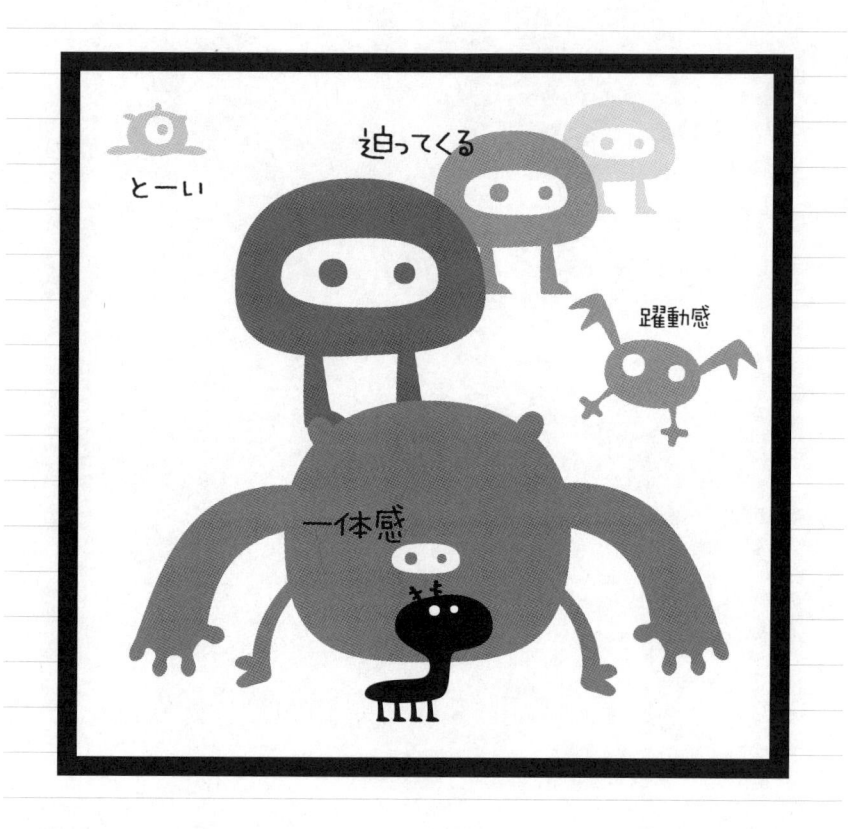

時表現ほど，感覚的な要素もあまりないでしょう。「現在時より前のことだから過去形」――そんな定義を離れて各表現を感覚としてつかんでください。「離れた」が自動的に「過去形」――心とことばをシンクロさせるんですよ。

PART 5

CHAPTER 16

時表現

TEMPORAL EXPRESSIONS

英語例文数：117　CDトラック数：09

時のない文

SECTION 1

CD track B-27

A 命令文 (☞P.545)

[a] Kiss me!

[b] Be quiet!

B 願望・要求・提案などをあらわす節 (☞P.545)

[a] I always insist that my staff be well dressed.

[b] They are demanding that she pay in cash.

[c] I propose that the money be spent on library books.

[d] It is important that you give 100% to your job.

SECTION 2 現在形

CD track **B-28**

A 現在を含め広く成り立つ状況 （☞P.547）

[a] I'm a student.

[b] I know 3 languages.

[c] Humans are social animals.

[d] Did you know that a hen lays about 228 eggs a year?
 — Who cares?!

B 現在の習慣 （☞P.548）

[a] My Dad catches the commuter train into the city.

[b] I practice karate really hard.

C 思考・感情 （☞P.549）

[a] I think it's a waste of time.

[b] I love chocolate crepes.

[c] His fans adore him.

PART 5 - CHAPTER 16 : 時表現

D 宣言 (☞P.549)

[a] I promise I won't be late again.

[b] I suggest you add more salt.

[c] I apologize for behaving like a jerk last night.

E 実演（今まさに展開していく状況）(☞P.550)

[a] I chop the carrot into small cubes like this.

[b] Watch carefully. First, I shuffle the cards like this. Then, ...

[c] Here comes the bus. Hurry!

F 現在形，その他のポイント (☞P.551)

[a] When you arrive at the hotel, please give me a call.

[b] If you exercise every day, you'll soon lose weight.

[ ] Janet: I was reading a book in bed last night when suddenly the room starts to shake and the lights go out. I freaked out!
Miyuki: Oh, that was just an earthquake!

SECTION 3 過去形

CD track **B-29**

A 丁寧表現 （☞P.555）

[a] I hoped you could lend me some money.
　→ I hope you can lend me some money.

[b] How many nights did you wish to stay, sir?

B 控えめな過去の助動詞 （☞P.556）

[a] This would be my 8th trip to Japan, I think.
　→ This will be my 8th trip to Japan.

[b] Geoff can/could fix it.

[c] I may/might have a quick drink with Terry on my way home.

C 仮定法 （☞P.557）

[a] I wish I had a girlfriend.

PART 5 - CHAPTER 16：時表現

進行形（be＋-ing）

SECTION 4

CD track B-30

A 躍動的な状況の描写 (☞P.559)

ⓐ My parents are holidaying in Kenya.
　→ 【現在形】 My parents often holiday in Kenya.

B 短期間 (☞P.559)

ⓐ I'm living in NY at the moment.
　→ 【現在形】 I live in NY.

ⓑ Which team are you supporting?
　→ 【現在形】 Which team do you support?

C 動詞との相性 (☞P.563)

ⓐ The bus was stopping.
　→ 【過去形】 The bus stopped.

ⓑ I think my poor cat is dying.

ⓒ The helicopter is landing.

ⓓ She was coughing.
　→ 【過去形】 She coughed.

ⓔ My husband was snoring noisily all night.

D 進行形・その他の表現効果：〜してばっかりいる （☞P.564）

a He is always picking his nose.

b My mother is constantly worrying about something or other.

現在完了形（have＋過去分詞）

PART 5 - CHAPTER 16：時表現
SECTION 5
CD track B-31

A 間近に起こったできごとをあらわす （☞P.566）

a. Oh my gosh, he has peed his pants!
   → 【過去形】 He peed his pants.

b. Look. It's stopped raining.

c. Have you heard from Geoff?

B 経験（〜したことがある）（☞P.567）

a. I've eaten fried ants.
   → 【過去形】 I ate fried ants.

b. I've enjoyed many fascinating adventures.

c. We've been to Machu Picchu.

C 継続（ずっと〜している）（☞P.569）

a. We've been partners for 3 years.
   → 【過去形】 We were partners for 3 years.

b. I've lived in Nagoya since 2001.

c. The M40 has been under construction for weeks.

ⓓ **How have you been?**

ⓔ **14 years have passed since I came to Japan.**

D 結果（「だから今…だ」という含み）（☞P.571）

ⓐ **I've dislocated my shoulder, so I can't play tennis.**
　→【過去形】**I dislocated my shoulder.**

PART 5 - CHAPTER 16：時表現

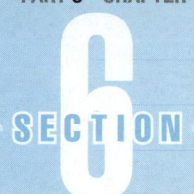

SECTION 6 完了形バリエーション

CD track B-32

A 過去完了形 （☞P.575）

[a] The poor man had already died when the ambulance got there.

[b] He wasn't in a good mood because his boss had ordered him to work overtime.

[c] Ben was over the moon. He had just got promoted.

B 助動詞 ＋ 完了形 （☞P.577）

[a] I will have finished my homework by 10.

[b] They will have arrived in Los Angeles by now.

[c] Something may have happened to her. I'm very worried.
　→ Something may happen to her.

[d] He must have forgotten to cancel the reservation.

[e] I should have studied harder.

C 現在完了進行形 （☞P.579）

[a] I've been cleaning the kitchen since this morning. I'm exhausted.

[b] I've been waiting for you for ages!

未来

A will の描く未来 (☞P.581)

[a] It will rain tomorrow.

[b] Hey, the movie starts in just 15 minutes.
— Don't worry, we'll make it in time.

[c] I'll give you a hand with the dishes.

[d] OK, OK, I'll clean my room!

[e] I think I've been given the wrong grade.
— OK, I'll check it out.

B be going to (＋動詞原形) の描く未来 (☞P.582)

[a] It's going to pour down any minute.

[b] Watch out! The boxes are going to fall.

[c] Look. He is going to do some magic.

[d] Hurry. We're going to be late for class.

[e] Are you going to attend the party?

[f] I'm going to check out the new bookshop.

[g] Lucy's going to prepare dinner tonight. Bring some stomach medicine!

C 進行形が描く未来 (☞P.585)

[a] I'm playing badminton at 3.

[b] I'm having lunch with Keiko on Thursday.

[c] She's flying to Singapore this Friday.

D 現在形のあらわす未来 (☞P.586)

[a] My birthday is next Tuesday.

[b] What time does this train arrive at Tokyo Station?

[c] His presentation begins at 1:30 p.m.

E will + 進行形（will be -ing）を使った未来 (☞P.587)

[a] This time next week, I'll be sunbathing on the beach.

[b] I'll be playing golf at 3.

F be to の描く未来 (☞P.588)

[a] **You're to finish your homework before watching TV.**

[b] **2 students from my class are to be awarded study-abroad scholarships.**

[c] **At my best friend's wedding, I met the woman who was to become my wife.**

SECTION 8 　仮定法

CD track **B-34**

B 仮定法の心理（☞P.591）

[a] I wish I had a girlfriend.

[b] If you kissed me, I'd scream.

[c] If you kiss me, I'll scream.

C 仮定法の作り方①：基礎（☞P.592）

[a] My car is really slow. I wish I had a Nissan GTR.

[b] Can you speak a foreign language?
　　— I wish I could.

[c] I wish I were/was richer.

[d] I wish I had been more attentive. Now I have to retake the class.

[e] I have a terrible bellyache. I wish I hadn't eaten so much chocolate!

PART 5 - CHAPTER 16：時表現

D 仮定法の作り方②：if を用いた仮定法文　(☞P.595)

[a] If you stopped smoking, you would feel much healthier.
　→ If you stop smoking, you will feel much healthier.

[b] If I were you, I wouldn't walk around that part of the city alone.

[c] If I had studied harder, I would have got a higher TOEIC score.

[d] If he had been less greedy, he would not have lost so much at the pachinko parlor!

[e] If you had followed the instructions, you wouldn't be in this mess now.

[f] If I had planned a bit better, everything would be fine.

SECTION 9 時制の一致

CD track B-35

A 時制の一致：基礎 （☞P.600）

[a] John said Ken loved Nancy.

[b] I thought Mary was really attractive.

[c] He promised me that he would never leave me.

[d] I heard that Judy had had another baby. Terrific news!

[e] I found out that she had lied to me. I was furious.

[f] The police said they had searched everywhere.

B 時制の一致と助動詞・仮定法 （☞P.603）

[a] She said she would go out with me, but she changed her mind.

[b] I told them we might be a bit late.

[c] What? But you promised you could finish the job by today.

[d] My Mom said I must be home by 11 p.m.

PART 5 - CHAPTER 16：時表現

[e] My doctor advised I should quit smoking.

[f] Rebecca said that she could make a pumpkin pie for the Halloween party.

[g] I said I wouldn't ask Gary because he's not reliable.

[h] He said he would buy me a diamond if he were rich.

[i] She wished she had a child.

C 時制の一致が起こらないケース (☞P.606)

[a] Our geography teacher taught us that Greenland is the world's largest island.

[b] Eri said her Dad plays mahjong every Saturday.

[c] Brian wrote that he will reach Kathmandu on April 1st.

ENGLISH GRAMMAR FOR 100 MILLION JAPANESE

PART 6
文の流れ
COMBINING SENTENCES

ながさにまけるな！

CHAPTER 17：接続詞
CHAPTER 18：流れを整える

PART 6　文の流れ

最後のパートは複数の文（節）をまとめあげ流れを作る練習です。例文もどんどん長くなりますが，その長さに慣れてください。「僕は女房を女王様みたいに扱ってるのに，絶対満足しないんだよなぁ」——この程度の文は居酒屋の酔っぱらいでも自由自在に繰り出しますよね。英語でも同じ芸当ができなきゃならないんだよ。絶対に負けるな。

PART 6

CHAPTER 17

接続詞

CONJUNCTIONS

英語例文数：40　　CDトラック数：02

SECTION 1 等位接続

A 順行の接続 (☞P.614)

■ and （〜と，そして）

[a] I made a sandwich and ate it quickly.

[b] It started to pour down, and we got soaked to the skin.

■ so （だから）

[a] I didn't use suncream, so I got burned.

B 逆行の接続 (☞P.617)

■ but （しかし・でも）

[a] I like my new boyfriend but hate his sense of dress.

[b] She never studies but always passes the tests easily.

[c] He is not just my friend but my soul mate.

[d] This car is not only powerful but (also) eco-friendly.

C 選択の接続 (☞P.620)

■ or（か・あるいは）

[a] You can pay in cash, or you can use a credit card.

[b] Which color do you want, red or blue ?

[c] 30 or 40 people attended the presentation.

[d] Hurry up, or we'll miss the train.

[e] We'd better do exactly as he told us, or else we'll be in deep water.

SECTION 2 従位接続

CD track B-37

A 条件 (☞P.622)

■ if (もし〜なら)

[a] If you wait a few minutes, I'll give you a ride.

[b] I know I can win if I play my best.

[c] I don't care if you have no money — I just like you!

[e] I don't know if Michelle received the package.

[f] He asked me if I have time for a drink.

B 理由（原因）(☞P.628)

■ because (〜なので)

[a] Because I didn't practice, I made no progress.

■ その他の「理由」をあらわす接続詞

[f] I went to bed very early, for I had had an exhausting day.

[g] Money is important in that we need it to survive.

[h] He was lucky inasmuch as they didn't fire him.

C 目的 (☞P.632)

[a] She stayed at work late so (that) she could complete the report.

[b] I have to be strict in order that the students realize who is the boss!

[c] I've organized the files such that each document will be easy to find.

D 譲歩 (☞P.633)

[a] Although/Though he was injured, he carried on playing.

E コントラスト (☞P.636)

[a] I support the Giants, while my girlfriend is a Hanshin Tigers' fan.

[b] The old system was fairly complicated, whereas the new system is very simple.

F 時間への位置づけ (☞P.637)

■ when (〜するとき)

[a] When I opened the overhead locker, a big bag fell on my head.

[b] I get nervous when I'm about to board a plane.

PART 6 - CHAPTER 17：接続詞

■ while（〜するあいだに）

[c] While I was driving to work, I felt a strange sense of déjà vu.

■ since（〜から）

[e] I've felt much better since we had that chat. Thank you!

G 多様な接続詞 as （☞P.640）

■① 同時（理由）

[a] I lost balance as I was trying to stand on my head.

[b] As the cost of air tickets has gone up so much, many people can no longer afford to travel.

[d] As time passed, his condition got better and better.

[e] As the unemployment level rises, the crime rate also increases.

■② 修飾する as:「〜として」

[a] As your doctor, I have to advise you to quit smoking.

[b] I regard my new job as a great challenge.

[c] Do as I say, not as I do.

[d] I paid my debts, as agreed.

[e] As you know, it's Tom's birthday next week.

PART 6
CHAPTER 18

流れを整える
── 代用・省略・注釈・レポート文テクニック

GOOD FLOW ── SUBSTITUTION・ELLIPSIS・
ANNOTATION・REPORTING

英語例文数：12　　CDトラック数：02

重なりを省く・注釈を加える

CD track B-38

A 代用 （☞P.647）

I think the students you have to be wary of are the really clever ones. Sometimes they are overconfident and question the teacher's decisions, believing they have every right to do so. One of the kids in my class did that, but I jumped on him immediately and told him in no uncertain terms I would not tolerate such behavior. That was the last time he did it!

B 省略 （☞P.649）

A: My Dad said he would drive us to the baseball stadium on Saturday, but he can't drive us ... . So now I have no idea who will take us.

B: Maybe my Dad will take us. Oh, no. He is playing golf this Saturday, and my older brother is playing golf ... too. How about Jerry? He has a car.

A: Jerry? Last time you asked him, he left us in the lurch.

B: That wasn't my fault.

A: I'm not saying it was your fault! I'm saying he's not reliable. He never has been reliable. Mmm ... I know, I'll ask Momomi, the girl I met while I was working at Cocos. She's not contacted me for a while, but she is still a good friend. Though she's not the ideal choice, she may, if she is asked nicely, help us out.

B: Well, you can try if you want to try. I don't have a better idea. Fingers crossed!

C 注釈を加える（同格・挿入）(☞P.651)

　　We heard a rumor that one of our teachers was being fired. Ms Williams, our English teacher, was every student's favorite. The rumor, fortunately, was false. She was leaving, it turned out, to get married!

レポートする

CD track B-39

A 2とおりのレポート（直接話法と間接話法）（☞P.654）

[a] Lucy said, "I love you."

[b] Lucy said she loved me.

B 再構成のテクニック（☞P.657）

[a] The boys promised that they would stop teasing the girls.

[b] My doctor advised that we should get the flu injection.

[c] The government warned that people should avoid traveling to that country.

[d] Many parents complained that the school fees were too high.

[e] She asked, "Do you like the movie?"
 → She asked me if/whether I liked the movie.

[f] She asked, "Where do you live?"
 → She asked me where I lived.

[g] He said, "Let's try again."
 → He suggested we (should) try again.

MEMO

あとがき

POSTSCRIPT

　ふぅ。お疲れ様。ずいぶんがんばっていただけましたね。もう十分英語を話す自信がついたのではないでしょうか。みなさんはすでに英語にある、あらゆる文の形・表現テクニックをマスターしています。あとは、実際に使ってみるだけ。

　いいかい、英語は僕たちにとって外国語。いきなり100%の英語が話せるわけじゃありません。うまく言えなかったり、言い淀んだりすることだってもちろんあるでしょう。負けないことだよ。負けないでできるだけ多くの英語を口から出すことが肝心です。もう基礎は十分。そうやってがんばっているうちに、必ずみなさんが夢みた英語力が身につくはずです。

　がんばってね。

　Well everyone, I hope you find that this CD helps make your English far more natural. Use it not just once. Use it again and again and repeat the examples ... with feeling!

　Enjoy and take care!

MEMO

すべての日本人に贈る――「話すため」の英文法

一億人の英文法 CDブック

発行日：2012 年 6 月26 日　　初版発行
　　　　2020 年 9 月30 日　　第 9 版発行

著者：大西泰斗／ポール・マクベイ
発行者：永瀬昭幸

編集担当：八重樫清隆
発行所：株式会社ナガセ
〒180-0003 東京都武蔵野市吉祥寺南町1-29-2
出版事業部（東進ブックス）
TEL：0422-70-7456 ／ FAX：0422-70-7457
URL：http://www.toshin.com/books（東進 WEB 書店）
※本書を含む東進ブックスの最新情報は東進 WEB 書店をご覧ください。

本文イラスト：大西泰斗
装丁：東進ブックス編集部
印刷・製本：シナノ印刷株式会社

※落丁・乱丁本は東進 WEB 書店のお問い合わせよりお申し出ください。
但し、古書店で本書を購入されている場合は、おとりかえできません。
※本書を無断で複写・複製・転載することを禁じます。

© Hiroto Onishi & Paul Chris McVay 2012
Printed in Japan
ISBN978-4-89085-546-9 C1082

東進ビジネススクール
『ビジネス英語講座』のご案内

ビジネスで、本当に役立つ英語力を。

相手の心を動かす交渉力とコミュニケーション。
そんな真の英語力を身につけるには──？

ビジネスパーソンに必要な英語力の基準。それは、相手の心を動かしリードできるかどうか。世界で通用する高いレベルのコミュニケーション、つまりは英語でビジネスができる交渉力を身につける講座が、東進ビジネススクールの『ビジネス英語講座』です。

日本人が苦手とするスピーキングは、講義＋マンツーマンレッスンでその力を伸ばします。サロン形式の英会話教室とも、受け身の学習スタイルとも異なる、"成果が見えるプログラム"です。また、ビジネス英語の土台を築く学習として、企業の昇格試験にも用いられるTOEIC®テストに対応した講座も設置しています。

受講に必要なPC環境・ご準備

* インターネットに接続可能なパソコンが必要です。
  ADSL・CATV・光などの広帯域インターネット接続サービスの利用（実効速度 3Mbps 以上）
  ※無線接続（ワイヤレスLAN・通信カード等を利用した接続）での動作保証はできません。
* OSは、Windows 8.1/ Windows 10 以上を推奨。 * Macintosh での受講はできません。
* 受講で使用する次の機器を受講生個人でのご準備をお願いしています。
  ウェブカメラ、マイク付きヘッドセット（オンラインレッスンで使用します）

上記推奨環境は更新される場合があります。最新の推奨環境はHPでご確認ください。

詳細やその他の講座・システムについて、ウェブサイトで公開中！　| 東進　ビジネス | 検索 |

社会人向け講座

『英語で提案・説得できる力』が身につきます。
東進だけの実践的なラインアップ。

講義＋発話レッスンで、ロジカルに話す力を鍛える

ビジネス英語 スピーキング講座（①, ②）

ビジネスで求められる
英語による「応答力」「問題解決能力」「発信力」が身につく

受講期間	受講形態	対象
1年間	在宅でのウェブ学習 ※学習開始時は、学習アドバイザーがサポートをいたしますのでご安心ください。	TOEIC® LR スコア 650 点以上の方 （*推奨の目安）

概要

本プログラムは、ビジネスパーソンの皆様がグローバルな仕事環境において、「英語によるコミュニケーション能力」を養成することを目的としたプログラムです。TOEIC®スピーキングテストのスコアを評価目標とし、その対策を通してスピーキング力を高める内容となっています。TOEIC®スピーキングテストのスコアと実際のスピーキング力の間には高い相関があると言われており、本プログラムで学習しスコアを伸ばすことが、実際のビジネスの場で本当に役立つ英語の修得につながります。

学習のプロセスでは、①慣用語句の反復音読や、②スピーチ原稿の音読・暗唱等の発話練習はもとより、③状況説明、④質問対応を瞬時に行う練習や、⑤理由や具体例を伴って自分の意見を述べる訓練を徹底して行っていきます。結果として、ビジネスで求められる英語による「応答力」「問題解決能力」「発信力」が身につきます。

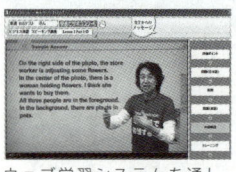

講義 [ウェブ] → **基礎トレーニング [ウェブ]** → **実践トレーニング [マンツーマン・オンラインレッスン]**

ウェブ学習システムを通し、いつでもどこでも受講可能。

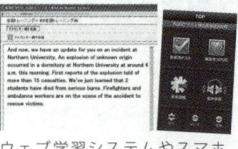

ウェブ学習システムやスマホアプリを使用して英単語などを集中的、効率的に修得。

ウェブ学習システムでのトレーニングや「TOEIC®新公式問題集」を用いたトレーニングを実行。

詳細やその他の講座・システムについて、ウェブサイトで公開中！ [東進 ビジネス] [検索]

講義＋英会話レッスンで、ネイティブスピーカーの感覚を理解しながら学べる

話すための英語 トレーニング講座

受講期間
1年間

受講形態
在宅でのウェブ学習
※学習開始時は、学習アドバイザーがサポートをいたしますのでご安心ください。

対象
TOEIC® LR スコア
基礎編：500点以上の方
実践編：700点以上の方　（*推奨の目安）

概要

本講座は、NHKの語学講座「ラジオ英会話」でおなじみの大西泰斗教授、ポール・マクベイ教授が担当。東進ビジネススクールの特別講師である2人の共著『一億人の英文法』（東進ブックス刊）をベースとした講座です。まずは英文を作り出すために必要な文法概念を講義で修得し、続いて音読や口頭英作文のトレーニングを行います。ノンネイティブで海外経験がない日本人でも、英語のネイティブスピーカーの感覚を理解しながら、言葉の意味やニュアンス、英文の作り方を学べる今までにない新しい講座です。

講義[ウェブ] → 基礎トレーニング[ウェブ] → 実践トレーニング[マンツーマン・オンラインレッスン]

学習項目：●とき表現：現在形、未来のwill ●基本文型：授与型 ●名詞の位置：主語、目的語 応用文型：itを上手に、it…を後ろから追いかける ●否定文：notを使う技術 ●修飾：修飾の2方向、-ing修飾・自由自在、to不定詞修飾・自由自在など

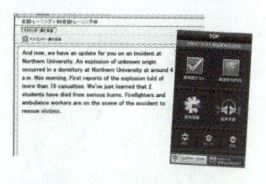

よりスムーズに発話をするためには、自主的なトレーニングが重要です。英単語の学習（PC＆アプリ活用）、ディクテーションの学習（PC活用）をすることで、瞬発力を高めます。

東進USAオンライン講師によるマンツーマンレッスンです。事前に専用サイトで予約をしておけば、アメリカ在住の講師が予約した時間にWEBシステムを利用して受講生にコンタクトします。「話せる」ための知識（発音、表現のニュアンスなど）を習得し、その知識をベースに発話訓練を行うスピーキング力強化講座です。心の意図を伝えるために、文法だけではなく、語彙、イントネーションなども学びます。

グローバルビジネスのスタートラインに立つ

TOEIC®テスト 800点突破講座

受講期間
年間

受講形態
在宅でのウェブ学習

対象
TOEIC® LR スコア
50点〜795点の方
（*推奨の目安）

英語の学び直し・土台固めに最適！

TOEIC®テスト 650点突破講座

受講期間
1年間

受講形態
在宅でのウェブ学習

対象
TOEIC® LR スコア
400点〜645点の方
（*推奨の目安）

詳細やその他の講座・システムについて、ウェブサイトで公開中！　東進 ビジネス　検索

大学生向け講座

世界にはばたく
リーダーとしての
「ビジネスコミュニケーション力」
を高める

TOEIC®は通過点!
テストの先に「世界で大活躍するための英語」がある。

　東進の『ビジネス英語講座』では、大学受験の英語から相手の「心を動かす」コミュニケーションへ、英語力を高めていきます。そのファーストステップとして、TOEIC®のスコアアップを狙う学習を進めることで、成果を感じながらコミュニケーション力を高める素地を作ります。
　そのうえで、さらに発信力を鍛えるトレーニングを重ね、未来のリーダーに必要な「世界で大活躍するための英語」の力を磨いていきます。

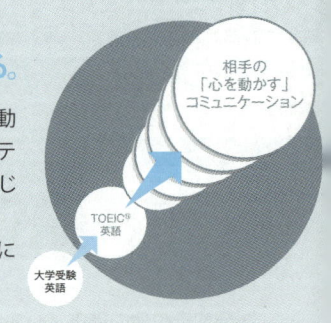

相手の「心を動かす」コミュニケーション

TOEIC®英語

大学受験英語

科学的な徹底訓練がスコアアップと実力向上を確実にします

4STEPを使い6か月で「英語力」を高める

東進ビジネス英語講座だけのカリキュラム

英語力を高める4ステップ学習法
- 概念理解
- 基礎トレーニング
- 実践トレーニング
- アセスメント

---

1 概念理解

映像授業

ルール・方法を学ぶ

語学習得は、スポーツ・楽器の習熟に例えられます。英語学習で最も大切な概念理解。スポーツでいえば、競技の基本ルールや方法論を学ぶステップです。東進では、実力講師による映像授業で実践的な英語を本質から理解し、それぞれのアセスメントで求められる英語の考え方・表現力・語彙力などを自分のものにします。一時停止、早戻し、最受講も自由自在。自宅や、大学授業の空き時間にも受講可能です。

Point 1. 高速学習
映像授業の長所を生かして毎日受講することができます。午前5時〜翌午前2時まで、21時間学習することができます。大学の授業やアルバイト等で忙しくても、両立して受講が可能です。

Point 2. 確認テスト
毎回授業後にある確認テストで知識・概念の定着を図ります。

受講 → 確認テスト → 次の受講へ

---

2 基礎トレーニング

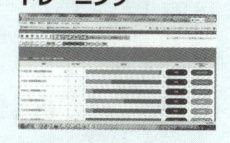

トレーニング

反復練習

理論に加えて、基礎的なスキルの修得も大切です。スポーツでも楽器でも、筋トレや地道な反復練習が欠かせません。TOEIC®テストの99.1%以上を網羅する高速基礎マスター講座で、語彙力と表現力を徹底的に磨きます。通学時間などのすき間時間をフル活用できます。

高速基礎マスター講座

Point 1. 「できない」問題をリスト化
未修得の単語・熟語を洗い出しリスト化して、弱点だけを修得することができます。暗記しやすい工夫がされているため、短期間で集中して覚えることができます。

Point 2. 定期的なトレーニング
短期集中で暗記しても定期的に活用しなければ、やがて忘却してしまいます。そこで、定期的にトレーニングや修了判定テストを実施することで、一度修得した知識を深めより確実なものにします。

---

3 実践トレーニング

TOEIC®トレーニング講座

受験テスト → 採点 → 解答解説 → (2回目)受験

何回も問題を解きなおすことで、問題形式に慣れ、得点が向上します。

東進USAオンライン講座

Point 1. レベルにあった実践練習
「オンライン英会話」のような「フリートーク」ではありません。受講する講座に応じて、本人のレベルにあった適切かつ実践的な課題を練習します。

練習試合

実践トレーニングは、スポーツの練習試合にあたり、これまでの授業やトレーニングで学んだことを実践します。TOEIC®形式問題でのトレーニング、教員資格を持ったネイティブスピーカー講師とのウェブレッスン&その場でフィードバック。最高レベルのマンツーマントレーニングを繰り返し行います。

---

4 アセスメント

TOEIC® LRテストまたはTOEIC® SWテスト

公式試合

東進では、毎月学習の成果を測ります。そのものさしとなるのが、公認のTOEIC® IPテスト(LRテスト、Sテスト、Wテスト)です。ETS世界基準で今の英語力を確認できます。

※テストはコースによって種類が異なります。

東進はオンラインが基本！
電車の中でも大学の空き時間でも学習が可能！

音声ダウンロード可能！
授業内で用いる音声を全てダウンロードできます。音声を聞きながら何回も音読・反復することで身に付きます。

詳細やその他の講座・システムについて、ウェブサイトで公開中！　東進 ビジネス　検索

東進ビジネス英語講座のTOEIC®スコアアップ実績

1年で平均116.0点アップ!!

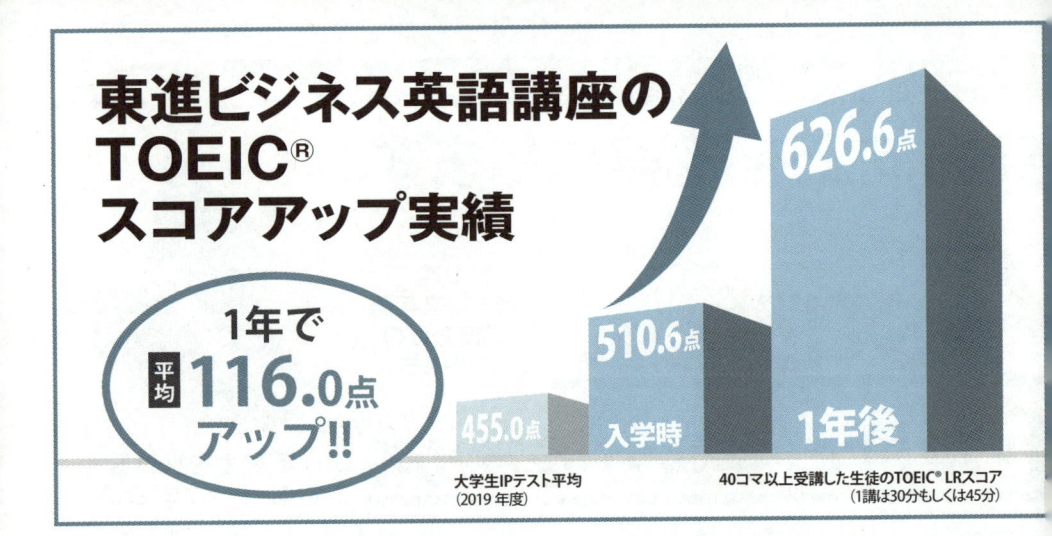

- 大学生IPテスト平均（2019年度）: 455.0点
- 入学時: 510.6点
- 1年後: 626.6点

（40コマ以上受講した生徒のTOEIC® LRスコア）
（1講は30分もしくは45分）

大学入学からスタートダッシュ！

藤生 竜季 くん　295点UP
555点（高校3年12月） → 850点（大学1年4月）
明治大学　理工学部

日々、大学の勉強（課題）の前に英語の勉強をする！

英語はこれからの時代に生きていくために絶対に必要です。私の専門の建築は、国内需要は減少の一途と聞きました。そこで海外で働きたいと考え、英語力を本気で伸ばすために大学に推薦合格した時点から東進ビジネス英語講座の受講を始めました。安河内先生の授業は「どうやったら楽しく英語を勉強できるか？」「大学生活を最大限に充実したものにするにはどうしたらいいか？」という事にも触れられており、英語学習や学生生活のモチベーションアップに効果的です。受講を進める中で、基礎が固まり、リスニングが得意になりました。英語を、日本語を介さずに理解できるようになり、英語のニュースを聞き、英語でその日の「やることリスト」を作成するなど、日常生活のほとんどを英語で行うことができるようになりました。

大幅スコアアップで夢に踏み出した！

真庭 里奈 さん　285点UP
640点（大学3年2月） → 925点（大学4年12月）
早稲田大学　基幹理工学部　卒業

東進の高速学習で競争率約100倍の採用試験を突破！

私はどうしてもパイロットになりたいという希望があり、採用試験までにTOEIC®の成績を上げる必要がありました。元々は東進卒業生ではありませんでしたが、幅広く教材・講座等を調べた結果、最も成果が出そうだと考え、東進ビジネススクールに入学しました。
成績が伸び悩む時期もありましたが、東進の高速学習を最大限に活用してスコアアップを実現しました。一緒に勉強する仲間の存在が、高いモチベーションの維持に繋がりました。この度、航空会社の競争率約100倍のパイロット候補生試験に合格し、夢への一歩目を踏み出すチャンスを得ることができました。

東進の英語コースでTOEIC®のスコアを着実に伸ばす！

資料請求・お問い合わせ：
右記のQRコードからお願いいたします

東進ビジネススクール

東進　ビジネス　検索
www.toshin.com/bs/

大学生の方　社会人の方

※講座内容は予告なく改訂される場合があります